Eucharist

The Meal and the Word

Ghislain Lafont

TRANSLATED BY
Jeremy Driscoll, OSB

Paulist Press
New York/Mahwah, NJ

Cover design by Sharyn Banks
Cover photo by Rhonda Watson
Book design by Lynn Else

Library of Congress Cataloging-in-Publication Data

Lafont, Ghislain.
    [Eucharistie. English]
    Eucharist : the meal and the word / Ghislain Lafont ; translated by Jeremy Driscoll.
        p. cm.
    Includes bibliographical references (p.   ).
    ISBN 978-0-8091-4459-4 (alk. paper)
    1. Lord's Supper. 2. Food—Religious aspects—Catholic Church. 3. Communication—Religious aspects—Christianity. 4. Language and languages—Religious aspects—Catholic Church. I. Title.
    BX2215.L3413 2008
    234'.163—dc22

                                                                    2007032615

Published by Paulist Press
997 Macarthur Boulevard
Mahwah, New Jersey 07430

www.paulistpress.com

Printed and bound in the
United States of America

Contents

Translator's Preface

The desire to present an English translation of Ghislain Lafont's *Eucharistie, le repas e la parole* has its roots deep inside a friendship: my friendship with Lafont's theology and my friendship with him. I first met him in 1980 when I was sent to Rome to study at Sant' Anselmo, the Benedictine athenaeum in the city. Sant' Anselmo houses monks from all over the world, and students and professors live the monastic life together as they go about their studies in the different ways their roles require. He became for me one of the master teachers of my life and also a cherished confrere in the monastic life, a guide on both counts, being my senior in the monastery by some thirty years. I took his courses and read his books; I lived with him and talked with him; and I was always greatly stimulated and marked by his profound and creative approach to the great classical themes of theology.

Some few of Lafont's books have been made available in English. I had always wished for more but never thought to set myself to the task of translating—until I read *Eucharistie, le repas e la parole*. I thought to myself that this book really must be known. Beautiful and profound in its own right, it is also a work of his mature years in which so many of the themes he pondered and wrote about for decades are all brought to bear on the Church's greatest treasure: the Eucharist.

Ghislain Lafont was already a distinguished theologian when he came to Sant' Anselmo in Rome in 1976. Nonetheless, his work in Rome during the next twenty years would more and more give shape to the theological project he was developing. At the same time, this work began to mark deeply the theological tradition of Sant' Anselmo. Bringing with him an approach to theology marked by the French schools and a tradition from his own monastery of La Pierre qui Vire, he began to mix and blend these with the international scene in theology and monastic life that he found in Rome. When I spoke with Lafont about what the move to Rome meant for him, he told me that he became increasingly aware of wanting to accomplish two things in the theology he was developing. First, he wanted to put into relief the relevance of the faith for the deepest longings of the human spirit, both on the personal level and on the level of culture. Second, he wanted to develop some of the fundamental intuitions of the Second Vatican Council, and thereby to contribute to the renewal of theology that the council called for. In this renewal he concentrated his attention especially on questions of history and symbols. For this work he brought to it what might be called a *typological eye,* that is, the capacity to discern and behold the great thought forms of an era, its controlling symbols. He brought a refined sensitivity for discerning a style and the styles in both theology and philosophy, tracing these through the history of each, letting the differences stand and finding the places where the differences can touch and communicate.

In the year 2000 Lafont's former colleagues and students at Sant' Anselmo honored him with a collection of studies entitled *Imaginer la théologie catholique.* This titled play on a work of his own called *Imaginer l'Église catholique.* No one, who knows the writings of Lafont, would deny that he has always brought imagination to the work he has done. In the 1950s, another book on the thought of St. Thomas Aquinas—Lafont's first major publication—certainly could have run the risk of being a book lacking in imagination, simply for sheer dint of Thomistic studies during the centuries. The fruitfulness of Lafont's approach, however, is shown in the fact that this book was reprinted as recently as 1996. But his grounding in Thomas is a key to understanding the nature of the creativity that Lafont brought to bear in subsequent studies. He once told me that at the time he wrote the book on Thomas, he thought that he would spend the rest of his theological life moving within that kind of scholastic theology. But then came Vatican II and the new impulse that the council brought to theology. Lafont took the inspiration and developed what he first learned in Thomas in the directions of a renewed theology.

This grounding in Thomas, combined with the new energy in theology at the time of the council, explains why Lafont's is a thoroughly Catholic theology. He let himself be challenged by the concerns of *aggiornamento*, by the Protestant critique, especially as represented in Luther's *teologia crucis,* and by the dialogue with contemporary philosophy, especially Heidegger. He was never afraid to accept what was valuable and true in what came to him from beyond the Catholic theological tradition. And yet he always brought his position into continuity with the deepest strands of the Catholic tradition, refreshing these for our changed situation.

In this Catholic tradition, Lafont is, naturally enough, a theologian under the rubric of faith seeking understanding. It can be considered a given in this rubric that the faith that comes to us from the apostles in its essence does not change. This fact is always a guide and an anchor for the theologian. But if such faith grows in understanding, especially under the impetus of and in dialogue with major new movements of thought, something will be transformed. "The Tradition that comes from the apostles makes progress in the Church," as Vatican II's *Dei Verbum* reminds us, "through the contemplation and study of believers..." (DV II, 8).

Lafont's theology can be, I think, justifiably described as christocentric, though it expands, under the force of what he finds in Christ, to trinitarian dimensions. I still love how much is suggested in the title of one of his books published in 1969, whose English title would be *Can God Be Known in Jesus Christ?* Yet in addition to the Christ and God questions, Lafont has devoted much time to thinking also about the Church and the nature and history of theology. Christ is always his concrete starting point, however, and indeed is the inspiration for the love and drive that one senses between the lines of all that he writes.

There is also a wholesome restlessness to Lafont's theological project, a restlessness that derives from an eschatological perspective. Whether it be the history of theology or current forms and structures in the Church, he will challenge his reader not to let himself be deluded into thinking that any past or present formulation or structure is the only possible one. But this challenge is not the challenge of a theological agitator. It derives from a profound and very personal spiritual sensitivity to the Church's waiting for Christ's return in glory. This permits him to launch responsibly whatever challenge he feels inclined to offer.

As for the present book, I think to offer readers just one clue to help them enter it with profit. I urge them to take note of the logic of the method and of the structure, which are at one and the same time simple and profound. The method, expressed in the structuring of the chapters, is first to think about basic human realities: what it means to eat and drink together (chap. 1), what it means to speak a word (chap. 2). Such reflection will show that these are amazing realities and that they mysteriously form the context in which the deepest desires of the human heart are expressed and hoped for. The next step of the method is to show how the Christian Eucharist is in fact the most profound instance of eating and drinking together and the most profound instance of speaking a word (chap. 3). Here what the human heart hopes for is realized. But there is in fact a precise content in what the eucharistic meal celebrates and what the eucharistic word says: it celebrates and says the death and resurrection of Jesus Christ. And so the same method returns: we must first reflect on what any death means and, in that light, on what the death of Jesus means. Only in this way can we also understand what resurrection might mean (chap. 4).

In his introduction Lafont explains why he pursues this method of analysis of the human reality and then its Christian shape: "to invite my readers to verify in themselves the humanity of their faith and of their sacramental experience." Finally, and typical of him, Lafont brings these fresh perspectives into dialogue with the theological language about Eucharist as classically conceived. What does it mean to speak of the body and blood of Christ, of the transformation of bread and wine into these? How does it come about? What can it all mean (chap. 5)? Again in his own words: "It is not a question of inventing something new but rather of putting a well known reality in a new light by taking different paths."

In a word, our most familiar human activities are transfigured in the Eucharist and bring us into life-giving contact with God in Jesus Christ. This fact dictates a method and a structure: we reflect on these activities—for they are not abandoned, they are transfigured—and we reflect on what happens to them in Jesus Christ. "The Eucharist: all at once feast and death, word of invocation and story, life and communion!"

Jeremy Driscoll, OSB

Introduction

Our human existence presents us with a certain number of concrete faces, with ways of acting, and with behaviors—that no authentic religion or wisdom tradition can ignore. Let us call these things "figures." Such figures—by which I mean *food, work, sexuality,* and finally, *death*—are either integrated, rejected, or transfigured, as the case may be. Corresponding to these are the human voice in all its registers and the human *word*—for example, invocation, story, the poem, law...These figures and words never cease to occupy us: they live in literature; they provoke the plastic arts, drama, and dance. Even cinema is precisely about these figures.

The figures call to one another. They respond each to the other and render the other fruitful. Yet no one of them is complete, that is, none completely satisfies the personal and collective desire of the human person. Each figure, and all of them together, point in the same direction; and the meaning of each is revealed in part by its similarity to and its difference from the other. None of them ever achieves a final or exhaustive performance. This is why they remain open, summoning what they signify and reaching toward some sense of "elsewhere" or "other." They themselves do not know and cannot produce what they reach for, but the elsewhere or other toward which they reach respond better than they can to what they are seeking. These figures seek a sort of universal communion that would transfigure them and that could be named with the all-embracing term *salvation*. Yet, reciprocally, this salvation is expressed through the mediation of these figures. Salvation is an eschatological feast, fountain of youth, food of immortality, mystical union, final repose. In negative terms, it is an end to suffering and the disappearance of death. The various religions and wisdom traditions, perhaps each in its own way, point to that "elsewhere" or "other" and propose ways of reaching it. These ways are in fact characteristic variants in the usage and practice of the figures and words common to all peoples. "Religion" especially makes use of the rite, that is, a certain symbolic usage of the figures of food, sexuality, and death, that corresponds to the memory preserved in a tradition. "Wisdom traditions" put the accent more on the ethics of behavior and the interiority of the desired salvation. Their emphasis falls on the word, especially law, and then, finally, on silence.

If we read the stories and the poems of sacred scripture with these symbols in our minds and hearts, we are surprised to find them on virtually every page. We have entered what Henri de Lubac called "the field of symbols." These renew the understanding of the sacred text. Now if this is the case with scripture, would it not also be so with the liturgy, and especially with the eucharistic celebration, the fundamental rite of the Christian religion? In fact, the Eucharist involves the use of *word,* especially in its modalities of invocation (prayer) and of memory (story). It takes up *foods* (bread and wine), referring them to the event of the *death* and *resurrection* of Jesus of Nazareth. Work and sexuality are not directly employed in the rite, but they are present along its edge. The food taken up is a product that has been transformed by human beings and is not simply a product of nature. As for the human and spiritual fruits hoped for from the celebration of the rite, this is readily expressed in the symbolic register of union—indeed, nuptial union—and it claims to reach the spiritual heights envisioned by wisdom. The reading of the Song of Songs once was a part of the elements that concluded the celebration, and the final prayers often refer to love. It is said that the Carthusians, after receiving communion, used to lean back in their choir stalls, the body bent and the head held up by a hand, as if in that moment the inspired words were fulfilled in them, "His left hand is under my head, and his right hand embraces me" (Song 2:6).

In the following pages, I want to attempt a reading of the Eucharist that takes its point of departure from these great symbols, symbols with which the human sciences have been so concerned in the last half century. Beginning with food, I will endeavor to trace the progression that moves from the simple act of eating to the celebration of a festal meal. I develop this reflection on food together with a reflection on language, precisely because the festal meal, if it is accompanied by joyful words, often concludes with a discourse addressed to the heroes of the feast. Such a discourse is a memorial of the past. With it we want to bring it back to life in its most fruitful moments and then to wish the hero a long life—indeed, a life that never ends.

On the basis on this analysis of food and language, I will examine what could be called *eucharistic discourse*. To whom is its language addressed? What does it remember? What does it hope for? Who pronounces it? What is its relation to the food that is shared? In this way we can return to the particular elements of the Eucharist in its relation to all other festal meals: (1) specifying what the Eucharist remembers—namely, the death and resurrection of Jesus (the level of language); (2) specifying what is given in the Eucharist to eat—namely, the body and blood of Christ (the level of food); and (3) specifying what is realized—namely, the Christian community awaiting its fulfillment (the level of finality) and invited both to universal love of others and to mystical union with its God.

The result of such research will obviously be classical. It is not a question of inventing something new but rather of putting a well-known reality in a new light by taking different paths. The Eucharist reveals itself to be the place of communion with God, founded on the memory of Jesus Christ, hoped for in its perfection in eschatological time, already realized in the symbolic celebration. Yet by the same token, it likewise reveals itself as the symbolic fullness of human existence. Its word is a permanent invocation that achieves a total expression, an expression both diachronic (saying the world) and synchronic (saying history). Its food is a total exchange of the food of immortality. The death of which it speaks is a total gift of self and a call to life. In all three cases there is love, that is, the twofold desire that the other be and that the other cause to be.

There were two ways in which this book could have been written: either "scientific" or "academic," or "meditative." I have opted for the latter. Initially the book was conceived through an encounter more than thirty years ago with Marcel Mauss' *Essai sur le don*. When I read this book, I experienced the kinds of reactions that Claude Lévi-Strauss describes and that I would like to cite here: "Few are they who have read *Essai sur le don* without feeling the whole range of emotions so well described by Malebranche evoking his first reading of Descartes: the heart beating, the head boiling, the mind invaded by a certitude (as yet indefinable but nonetheless dominating) that you are present at a decisive event of the scientific evolution."[1]

The "trance" in question derived certainly from the intriguing content of the *Essai*. But I also had an intuition that here was a perfect instrument for entering into a new and joyful meditation on the Christian Eucharist and something that perhaps promised a renewed practice of it. Thus I became involved in research that was intellectual and, at the same time, oriented in a Christian way. The theme of *exchange* that emerges in Mauss' work can be considered a sort of key for reading all that was discussed in the eighties in the human sciences and in philosophy. That discussion moved from Lévi-Strauss to Baudrillart, from Derrida to Lacan and Levinas, together also with Paul Ricoeur. It moved across different levels: the level of things, human beings, liberty, and language. It registered irreducible diversities,[2] both positivist and spiritualist. It was colored by despair, cold lucidity, or hope. There was an unceasing investigation concerning the structure, the mechanisms, and finally the sense of the symbolic as the space of encounter or of reciprocity. And all this took place against the background of a Marxism that had not yet slowed in its momentum. The rapid disintegration of Marxism contributed perhaps to exposing a certain lack of real referent in these investigations, however passionate they were. And because of the sustained refusal of any metaphysic, there appeared at length on the scene the era of emptiness, the *pensiero debole,* the return of the religious and what was called the "spiritual" search.

In the interval, however, Christian theology allowed itself to be instructed by the notion of the gift and by the weight of humanity that such a notion could contain. A correct restoration of thought, of art, and of ritual could perhaps unfold if contemporary culture, for its part, would be willing to understand a little of what the Christian tradition could offer it concerning both the covenant and the realism of creation. I have in mind here not only theological but also cultural contributions, namely, proposals like that of Louis-Marie Chavet, *Symbole et sacrement* (1986), or also the steady work of the Liturgical Institute of Padua, with the recent but already noteworthy contribution of Andrea Grillo and his *Teologia fondamentale e Liturgia* (1995), as well as the subsequent volumes. And in the year 2000, Maurice Bellet published his *La Chose la plus étrange: Manger la chair de Dieu et boire son sang.*

In the foregoing paragraphs I indicate the general climate in which I have tried over the years to reflect on the Eucharist and toward which I attempted to draw the attention of my students. I did this, of course, without neglecting more classical approaches. Here, however, I am only proposing a relatively brief essay that I offer as a kind of "meditative theology." It is *theology* to the extent that what I have written derives from long hours of grappling with authors, some of whom I have mentioned above, and concerning whom I could express my debt in lengthy pages of discussion, complete with scholarly notes. It is *meditàtive* because I have decided against the scholarly notes in order to offer instead a reflection that in places may seem naïve or too simple. The reason for this is that I would like to invite my readers to verify in themselves the humanity of their faith and of their sacramental experience. Reciprocally, I invite them to let the Christianity latent in their most simple gestures see the light of day, gestures such as taking food or addressing a word to another. With such gestures we try to go to the depth of every human person's desires and the hopes implied by them. So this is not a book designed for quick reading but rather an invitation to an interior journey toward oneself and one's symbols, as well as toward the community that engenders this symbolic life, toward other human beings who search for meaning, and toward God, who ultimately bequeaths it.

Notes

1. *L'Essai sur le don* has been republished in M. Mauss, *Sociologie et Anthropologie* (Paris, 1950), 143–279. The words of Lévi-Strauss are taken from the Introduction of this same volume, p. 33.

2. Just to take the example of food—this could be considered from the following points of view: descriptive, structural, psychoanalytic, baroque, erotic, aesthetic, or symbolic. There are overlappings among these approaches but also irreconcilable differences. And the same could be said about the discussions concerning language, sex, and death. So it will not be a question here of going to the depths of these discussions and differences. The method will necessarily be eclectic. On the one hand, theology and the eucharistic celebration itself will suggest in a more or less conscious way a choice within this forest of interpretations, while, conversely, some point of view from the scientific investigation will throw a new light on the eucharistic mystery.

CHAPTER ONE

Eating and Drinking

Food: Substance and Symbol

"From certain aspects, the real is at first sight simply food."[1]
This striking phrase shows us, as we undertake to speak
about food, that food is inseparably both substance and
symbol. It is *substance* because it is, first of all, food that
reveals to us the effective consistency of reality. In this sense
we speak of a "substantial meal," and such an expression
evokes a volume, a weight, and a materiality that are not the
whole of food (or of reality), but without which there would
be no food (or reality). It is *symbol* because the contours and
the materiality of the food are immediately taken up within
a network of meanings and values in which transpositions or
"metaphors" are produced and reproduced in a seemingly
endless game. This polarity of substance/symbol, manifested
first of all in food, seems fundamental to all the levels of
anthropological research. I begin this chapter with the crude
fact of food in order to throw into clear relief that end of the
pole concerning substance, which food reveals. To a certain
extent, this pole governs symbols and even words. I begin
here also in order to avoid a temptation rather common to
the human mind (and perhaps especially to the mind in its
theological function)—the temptation to forget the mind's
reference to the earth and to lose contact with that which
nevertheless constantly nourishes the variations of the imag-

ination. Too often, contact with the earth finds itself transposed into a bodiless conceptuality.

SUBSTANCE

Eating and drinking are primordial actions and initial recognition of the world. Before even her eyes are open or her legs trained for walking on the earth, the human infant eats or, more precisely, she drinks. By his very first gestures the infant subscribes to his body, which is earth and water; and inscribes it into the continual cycles of these first substances. Before she can offer any resistance, she opens her mouth and places it on the breast, which is for her the first nourishing opening in the earth. The infant greedily sucks up that which it can take as the real, and eliminates what has not been assimilated. From the start, from the first milk absorbed, but also at the end of life, with the last fruit juice painfully swallowed, a consubstantiation between the earth and the body and between the body and the earth is being worked out and is never interrupted. Absolutely nothing is done in our lives if not in counterpoint to this primordial and always active relation. Pleasure first takes place here where, following biological rhythm, we take from the earth and from water their substance to make it our own, and where we return to them what has not been assimilated. Nutrition is the live presupposition of every existence. When it becomes difficult, as when food is seriously lacking or even when a rhythm of consuming to which we have become accustomed is interrupted, hunger dislodges every other need and draws our attention back to this first existence. The smallest crust of bread is consumed with an attention that would seem almost a liturgy.

Were it possible, it would be necessary to enter here into the mysterious distinction between *solid* (what we eat) and *liquid* (what we drink). Earth is more familiar to us, and eating reassures us. The earth is support for our feet and holds firm under our sitting. It is an object for our hands, material for our work, chewable finally for our jaws, and substance for our food. Since it resists, it can be taken up and tamed by the very struggle directed toward it.

Water, on the other hand, is more elementary. It eludes our grasp; it is something living and flowing. Or it is hidden: deeper than the earth with its springs unknown, higher than the sky and we know not how to make it fall. Either because it slips away from us or because it can overwhelm and submerge us, water is hostile. And yet it is even more desirable than the earth; no doubt, because it is more elemental. Rather hunger than thirst!

Yet the distinction between solid and liquid has even more disquieting dimensions. A solid needs to be destroyed in order to be absorbed. It is necessary to bite, then chew, not to mention to undertake the destruction that precedes this. Plants have been picked, yanked from the earth. Animals have been put to death. The various operations of cooking, to which we shall return, have also attacked the living in order to render them edible, before human teeth complete the transformation. Some ancient civilizations had rituals that in some way asked pardon from the earth or from the animal for the murder that they were about to commit. Conversely, such a destructive act was considered access to a possible communication. If we assimilate what we eat, we are also assimilated to it; and a sort of mystical communion can be established. Cannibalism finds its ultimate explanation here.

Liquid, at first glance, appears less tragic. There is no biting or chewing. Human activity is not required to transform it. It is taken in and swallowed. And yet, what requires the least work seems the most necessary. Drinking is primordial;

eating follows only after. And everything must be more or less liquefied in order to be swallowed.

With this kind of talk we are not far from the Eucharist. In the Gospel of John, Jesus is not afraid to press the point. When his hearers recoil before his injunction that it is necessary to eat his body, he reiterates the point with an even stronger word; he speaks of "chewing" it. And he adds the command to drink his blood. I wonder if the long disuse of the practice of taking communion from the cup may not be explained in part by a kind of religious horror before the injunction that bids us to take such a drink. In any case, as regards the body, it was, up until a short time ago, presented under the form of an extremely refined host, which one dared not touch with the teeth, just as once it was not permitted to touch it with the hand. In this way, the body was dematerialized in the extreme, virtually liquefied; and the blood was left aside. The destructive dimension of biting and chewing was almost totally effaced.

Jesus said, "Take and eat." But there was no taking anymore, and there was scarcely any eating. The sacrament as such was reduced to nearly nothing for the sake of a content that was all but cut off from it. In their bodies people were kept at the greatest possible distance from the mystery to which they were nonetheless invited. From the Baroque period, down to our own times, all the realism of the Eucharist was centered not on the act of eating but on the real presence of Christ in that which was eaten. A sort of physical realism, which was more strongly affirmed the more we were distanced from it, gave way to considerations and prescriptions that have little to do with the truth of the sacrament. Behind all this is a conception of the Christian religion that penetrates the faithful without anything being said. Instead, it would be worth bringing to light to what extent we have been marked by the Eucharist now that we in fact chew the body and drink the blood. A liturgical reeducation is required that has hardly begun.

THE VOLUNTARY AND INVOLUNTARY DIMENSIONS IN EATING

Our relation to food is not limited to the actions by which we take it in. There is also digestion. This remains practically beyond the reach of what we decide upon, and if all goes well, even beyond our awareness. The most interior and most vital dimension of nutrition, that in which the union between food and ourselves is realized, takes place beyond our own powers. The passive form of the verb *to nourish* is required here; and it can be noticed, with just a little attention, that the human being, like all animals, is a relay in the rhythms of living material over which, in fact, we are not in charge.

The elimination of what is not assimilated, if taken into account, can constitute an inverse symbolic pole. Yet, this too escapes our power to decide. Meanwhile its possible inconstancy lets us glimpse the mysterious resistances put up in the way of our becoming truly human beings.[2] Paradoxically, this involuntary dimension of nutrition, which underlines the substantial pole of eating, points toward the ultimate mysteries of humanity and the cosmos. Paul Ricoeur, in *Fallible Man: Philosophy of the Will,* has said, "At a certain level of my existence, I am a problem resolved by a wisdom wiser than me. A wiser wisdom because the activity that it does 'all alone' produces, in the order of bodies, that which I could not do by myself of my own will, with my own brain, or with my own hands." And again, "Life builds life, the will only constructs things; the spectacle of life always humiliates the will." Yet rather than being humiliated by the spectacle of life, it would be better to decipher the sign and marvel at it. This could be the moment of trying to recognize in the life that we do not produce the trace of a presence, the moment of perceiving that the "biological" could be the place of the manifestation of the "transcendent."

An acquiescence to a superior wisdom acting within our bodies permits us paradoxically to recognize ourselves in our self-awareness and in our freedom. The way is given us, and the mixture of freedom and the involuntary in our bodily functions is like an invitation to acquiesce also where we are masters of our movements, to acquiesce to the superior wisdom that directs both the world and our bodies inserted in the rhythms of the cosmos. In this way the image of eating can become the symbol of a most intimate relation with God, in which God takes and always maintains the initiative. If we think now of the sacrament of the Eucharist, the fact that the consecrated species follows the same path as all other food is in itself the symbol of a kind of inverse transformation: a total transformation is indeed worked through the phenomenon of eating, but it is the faithful who are transformed into what they have received and not the contrary. They become in fact, together with all who eat it, the body of Christ.

FOOD AND LANGUAGE

Thus we have arrived very quickly at the symbolic pole of eating, though in fact we were already there. Our language itself, whose origin we often forget, leads us to the memory of earth, water, and food. The first experience of eating and drinking shapes the content of our first words and first phrases. It is this experience that evokes the expression of desire. All cultural developments are fastened to this, in play with the other two primordial layers of sex and death. The human being is so completely living flesh that the language of the flesh seems suited to say everything and to suggest what cannot be said. It is thus that we speak, beyond earthly foods, of food for the spirit or for culture; therefore we have a foretaste of the beyond in speaking of "a drink of immortality or of a feast without end." We also use such expressions as "taking a bite out of life, being starved for friendship, digesting an insult, swallowing your anger, chewing on an idea, devouring with the eyes…" And these are simply examples from current speech. We should also turn our attention to slang or to mystical language. It is in slang that the essential symbols come so spontaneously to the surface.[3] It is mystical language which transposes the key to the infinite degree but without uprooting the words from their earthly soil.

Concerning Cultural Foods

FOOD AND WORD

Edible earth and drinkable water respond to the human being, who is hunger, thirst, and appetite; and their interplay establishes a real undistanced consubstantiation between the world and the human being, even while it gives rise to a whole distanced network of metaphors and meanings. But there is also another distance, just as fundamental, which, stemming from the play between the word of request and the word of gift, places substantial food all at once in the world of culture. The human infant, unlike other infant animals, cannot approach by himself the breast that will be instinctively offered him. The mother must pick him up, perhaps also speaking tender words to him. And if the interval is too long between the feedings, the infant will cry out, which is to say he too will speak and ask in his own way. Culture is completely contemporaneous with nature, and here too there is a coexistence of substance and symbol. Never did the human race know a moment of pure animalness.[4] The mouth that eats learns in some way to insert itself between the mouth that asks and the ear that listens; and a little later in the life of the infant that mouth will learn as well the relay of the hand. It is at birth that incest is prohibited and feeding measured, which is to say, distributed within the limits of a certain legality, however limited. Our relation to the world is not enclosed within the circularity of the elements and the mobility of matter. It is inscribed within the word exchanged. By the same token, no word is ever totally cut off from some substantial foundation, for no matter how sublime an exchange may be, it always involves, more or less directly, the body.

This is perhaps the place to note a first religious pole to food. Food can be called *sacred* to the extent that the human being, who needs it, does not create it and so always receives it. This is true even if it must be produced, as we shall see shortly. Food is "taken" from the earth, which is rich with it. In some way one asks earth for it, either asking her as a sort of primitive deity, or asking the gods who have power over earth and water. Indeed, one is asking the food itself in so far as it is living and is going to die, and in the asking there is some sense of the need for reparation for the injury it is about to undergo. From this point of view food and sacrifice are not two separate realities. Since it is necessary to kill in order to be nourished, this implies that in some way or other this "murder" must be compensated. This is all the more true when the death is real or when the human role—as transformer and so as destroyer—is greater. The same holds true for the use of fire in cooking. Fire also comes close to sacrifice. These givens are orchestrated in any number of forms, but always in such a way that in the end cooking and sacrifice, the political city and the world of the gods, are entwined together and in that way articulated.[5]

THE RHYTHMS OF EATING: FASTING AND BULIMIA

There is a problem of truth and rhythm in eating, and it is part of the task of being human to resolve it. I will try to analyze briefly the various facets of this problem, but it would certainly be legitimate to say here, by way of introduction to our analysis, that Jesus and his mother were without doubt the only people who were completely successful in the task—so difficult yet so simple—of eating in the right way. The meals taken day after day with Christ were undoubtedly an important part of the education of his disciples. If it is true that "no man has ever spoken like this man," it is perhaps even truer that "no man has ever eaten like this man." Jesus ate and drank—and the Pharisees would have done well to do the same instead of reproaching him!—he also sometimes fasted, and very severely.

Fasting manifests our distance from the world that feeds us, and it corrects the tendency to take for ourselves what should always be considered as asked for and given. Fasting indicates certain essential dimensions of food. It indicates, first, the other; for a person rarely eats alone, and when there is want, food is shared. Next it indicates one's own self, not only the mouth but the hand and the ear. It indicates that which awakens desire, beyond the elements and other human beings. In this sense fasting activates the symbolic dimension of food without destroying its effective consistency. This is why fasting is essential for human beings, and it is also why it is difficult to find the right rhythm. It is a matter of signifying all the dimensions of desire. But this does not mean to place desire in conflict with the body, for this would be a refusal to be human (in order to become God?), indeed, a refusal of our primitive consubstantiation. In the garden of Eden God gave our first parents all the trees, which were not only "beautiful to see" but also "good to eat." Yet concerning them, he also said of one tree, "You shall not eat of it." Food and fasting will thus be the two poles of a correct relation to food.

This polarity is fragile and threatened from every direction, in particular by gluttony. Gluttony perhaps is the inverse of a poorly conceived fast. Instead of emphasizing the cultural and symbolic distance, the glutton throws himself avidly on substance. The sense of necessary participation in the materiality of the world is too lively, and the fear of being in want is too strong. The glutton manifests insecurity and develops an animal desire to subsist that expresses itself inappropriately on the most primary level of action: eating or drinking. Correlatively, gluttony or alcoholism can arise from the deprivation of correct symbolic and cultural relations in other domains in which, moreover, the body is involved. Deprived of symbol and exchange, a person can become involved in food without any discretion. When it is a question of appreciating the pleasure of eating and the quality of some particular food, however, be it just a genuine piece of bread—ever rarer in our day—then this is not gluttony but humanity. In whose name is it claimed that it is not human to enjoy what is good and what is offered us? Wasn't the wine that Jesus gave at Cana the very best that had ever been tasted? And yet the gospel leads us to understand that the banqueters had already reached their limit when Christ gave them his wine. Admirable invitation, this, to the pleasures of life! Perhaps even too much. Mental anorexia and bulimia, fasting, and the glow of the banquet! It is all a question of limits to transcend or to respect, of humans' concrete discernment, together or alone, of their real condition, which is composed of dependence and mastery alike.

Production, Cuisine, Consumption

PRODUCING

The Human Being and the Body before Food

Human beings eat. They eat from almost everything, and they are not spontaneously limited to one category of foods, such as only plants or only animals. And yet, in most cases nothing is eaten that has not been produced and prepared. Eating does not exist apart from work. Moreover, in producing as well as in eating human beings are not alone. Everything is done together spontaneously. Eating is social.

Karl Marx (*German Ideology,* Part I) reminded us: "Men begin to distinguish themselves from animals when they begin to produce their own means of existence, a step forward which is the very consequence of their material organization." Certainly, reflection will lead us quickly to distance ourselves from Marx; for "producing," which he calls a consequence of humanity's material organization, seems to surpass this materiality, from which it, nonetheless, in a certain sense, proceeds. First, however, it is worth recognizing the accuracy of his intuition and the truth of his formulation. This will help us to avoid falling into an idealism that is perhaps attractive but too facile. Human organization—this means our material makeup—is in one sense so new with respect to what immediately precedes it, that it liberates forces irreducible to all that had previously been manifested. Humans produce because they stand upright. Our hands are not necessary to our mobility. We are neither four-footed nor four-handed; our legs are sufficient to hold us on the earth and to move us around, while our arms and our hands are entirely free to do other things, to do real work: to gather, to cultivate, to transform. Culture, in its original sense of referring to agriculture, proceeds from the manual freedom that we possess, itself a consequence of being able to stand upright. But culture proceeds as well from the mouth and from the tongue, for the same reason that it proceeds from the hands. For it is together that the forelimbs and the face are set free by the upright stance. We no longer need our mouth to grab at foods from the earth. These now are brought to the mouth by the hand, which has perhaps also prepared them for easier chewing. The mouth and the tongue are thereby set free for the word, which corresponds to the cry of animals in the same way in which human technique, even the most simple, corresponds to the gesture of the animal's paw or the monkey's hand. Technique and word are born together, no doubt because they are destined to develop together since both derive from a unique physical configuration: the human being in the upright stance. We can add to this one further thought: at the same time that the hand was set free and the mouth became autonomous, the cervical capacity and the nervous mass reached their highest developments. It is as if the vital commands of this unique organism, the human body, were all at once ready for harmonious execution.

Paths in Anthropology

The "step forward" of which Marx speaks indeed comes from a material transformation of the human being compared to the other animals. But if this transformation is the result of a continuous movement—that prodigious move-

ment of the liberation of living beings in relation to their surrounding milieu, from the fish, entirely enveloped in the
water that sustains its body, all the way to the human being
standing upright on the earth—it nonetheless inaugurates a
new regime. In one sense all this striving toward the upright
stance seems, in a sense, to have been completed because the
vertical has been attained and it enables operations that, on
the level both of the brain and of the mouth, on the level of
the tongue and of the hand, are completely new and cannot
be explained by its pale prefigurations in the animal world.

In fact, to the extent that it is opposed to the predatory
instinct, the capacity to produce supposes a certain retreat in
relation even to that which is produced. There is a retreat of
the human person in respect to his or her own body to evaluate its needs and a retreat in respect to cosmic matter as a
whole in order to figure out how to produce something from
it. Because they stand upright, humans can adjust their relation to the earth, reflect on it, and plan for it. From this they
become aware not only of the fact that they produce but also
of their capacity to adapt, to invent, to know. This novelty,
which in one sense is certainly a consequence of material
organization, is in another sense irreducible because this
material organization can be reflected on and comman-
deered for work. If next we think from the point of view not
of production but of consumption, it is clear that this too
does not finish with eating, however primordial consumption may be. Humans discern within themselves other open-
ings, and the nourished body aspires to other things. Here all
the paths of culture find themselves intertwined.

Thus human "material organization" opens from within
itself a space that does not lead to the "material." It is precisely here that we become aware of the problem of being
human. There is a "problem" because the human being per-
ceives that he or she is body, but from the very fact that this

is known, one grasps that no one is only body. The sole means then of avoiding a dualism (speaking of a "super-structure" that is entirely extrinsic) is to recognize a distance interior to human beings themselves and constantly to evaluate the poles without separating them or confusing them.[6]

Poles of Anthropology

These several observations offer us a reading grid that lets us find our bearings amid the diversity of ways of being human. It is possible to think of the human being "from one of three ends": the *hand,* which indicates a relation to the material and a *technical* reference that, in a sense, cannot be exceeded; the *mouth,* which leads us to think of a human as a being of *language* and *communication;* and the *brain,* which continually places in image, memory, and thought the materials that come to it from concrete experience. In turn the brain orients this experience by the symbols and the directions furnished to it. This fact leads us to think of a human as a being of *significance.* If it is inevitable, however, that a person will begin from one or the other of these ends, it would be an error to reduce the picture to that one end or to condemn what emerges from the others. The "thinking reed" does not want to remember that it is still a reed or to honor in itself that which is not thought. The "logical" human, a being of language and of politics, despises the artisan, the metaphysician, and the artist. The "manual" human never stops being suspicious of the "superstructures," however inevitable they are and essentially rooted in him or her. These attitudes, fairly spontaneous in so far as we are not entirely reconciled with ourselves as human beings, express themselves readily by those words that end in -"ism," which indicates their ideological character. But "-isms" do not express the truth of the human person. This happens more often than is admitted; for after all, the harmonization of a diversity like ours is a long work. What is essential is to recognize that from whatever pole the question is approached, that pole is intrinsically affected by the characteristics of the other two.

So, if human beings eat, nothing reaches the mouth that is not the fruit of their power and technical imagination, and of their aesthetic sensibility as well. They eat nothing that is unmarked by the social situation of which language is the instrument. Conversely, the food they eat is thoroughly symbolic and expresses a great deal more than the satisfaction of an agitated appetite. "Tell me what you eat, and I'll tell you who you are." And if there is in us a desire that rises higher than the hand and mouth, then why should food in its own way not signify that desire? And why should that not also pertain to religious symbolism? Once again, it is in its relation to that threefold functionality—brain, face, hand—that human activity and all its objects reveal their true range.

PREPARING

Cooking

Technical capacity intervenes as early as the simple, initial steps of picking and gathering. Even at this level there is a certain preparation. Even things that will be eaten raw are not consumed without being washed and cut. Obviously a qualitative threshold is passed when preparation puts the "four elements" to use, letting humans experiment with their power, especially where the use of fire and water is concerned. I alluded above to the religious value—sacred and even promethean—of the preparation of food. It would be necessary here to turn to the precise and difficult analyses of Lévi-Strauss concerning "cooked and raw." He distinguishes foods put in direct relation to fire ("roasted") from foods in which water mediates between fire and the food ("boiled"). Boiling further requires the mediation of a vessel, this too being a work of human technique. And the invention of technical means goes hand-in-hand with their symbolization.[7]

Let it suffice here to note that by this activity, at once technical and sacred, the natural food becomes a cultural food. The given substance is manipulated to respond to the taste of people and to their need, to express their power or to signify their dependence in relation to the forces themselves that they use. In this way, food not only nourishes but, once prepared, it experientially reveals to people their humanity. Cooking thus appears as an active mediation between humans and nature. Before the process of humanization is totally realized by the absorption (and the destruction) of the food, a preparation is accomplished through both invention and docility. Cooking is a search for right combinations. People try different ways of treating the real; they continually confront these with their personal reaction and that of their group, but also with the possibilities revealed to them and with the resistances they encounter in the reality manipulated. Now, what holds true on the level of the products of the earth extends to all the dimensions of human existence. Culture is the collection of these processes of invention and adaptation, transmitted and enriched or forgotten and weakened, throughout the course of time, where each can signify and symbolize the other.

Division of Labor

Production and preparation also reveal a social dimension. Concerning the so-called primitive civilizations, operating on the reduced scale of a small community confined within a limited territory, it can be noted that some in the community are occupied with providing food and "producing" it, either by gathering, fishing, or hunting, or by procuring it through elementary exchanges. Others put these things together and prepare them. There are tasks preferred by one group or the other, by one sex or the other, even if the division of tasks differs considerably from one civilization to the next. I have the impression that, when the concrete modes of the division of labor throughout the ages are analyzed, it is necessary to conclude, in the last analysis, that this division is grounded in the biological roots of the race. The first major division of labor is between the sexes. As André Leroi-Gourhan notes, "The slow growth of the infant makes women naturally less mobile, and on the basis of its double feeding, there appeared for the primitive group no other solution than that the men hunt and the women gather" *(Gesture and Speech)*. We can wonder if culture here doesn't consist of intervening in nature in such a way that without dissolving the distinction between the sexes, that distinction does not result in a segregation that defines the role of each exclusively in terms of greater or lesser mobility.

The other division of labor derives from the level on which the activities of each person are exercised. The same person cannot develop brain, mouth, and hand all on the same level. Which of these three is developed defines not only one's productive capacity but also cultural orientation, allegiances, and the range of the symbolic. It is perhaps inevitable that this specialization will bring in its wake antagonism among the groups, and it is probably here that the roots of the "social question" lie. But this needn't constitute a static hierarchy, as Plato would have it, where the one (the philosopher) who thinks (brain) dominates the person (the politician) who speaks (mouth), who in turn enslaves the one (the peasant, the worker) who works (hand). The problem would perhaps be to find institutions that effectively recognize, in principle, the equality of the different functions, for they all arise from what we are, and they all favor communication between the groups that exercise them.

Competition and the Service of All

Let us return to our meal. The extension of interhuman relations in our day has created a situation in which, even for the smallest part of production and preparation, competition is required among workers across the whole globe. To be convinced of this, it is enough to give a little attention to the geographical origin of the foods we consume in a single meal and to take note of the origin of their packaging. The word *origin* here means not only what part of the earth it comes from but also the human persons who have worked to produce it, as well as those who have packaged it. No matter how gigantic the dimensions of structures and organizations have become, no matter how selfish they may be, a collective fundamental intention, today as before, cuts across the whole of human labor; namely, the intention of "procuring foods" and thus of procuring the life of the whole assortment of peoples, from within differentiated societies. This intention is present in the smallest piece of bread we eat. And the unbearable drama is that the distribution of these foods is so unequal. To drain off the majority of foods to a minority of people goes against the very being of the human race in its biological, technical, and social reality. What kind of revolution would be necessary to change this state of affairs? Whatever it might be, we cannot avoid the sign of responsibility invisibly marked on the food that comes to us from the earth and from human labor. If "humans begin to distinguish themselves from animals when they begin to produce their own means of existence," their food is, in its origins, a question of ethics.

Aesthetic Sensibility

It is also a question of the aesthetic. Why is it that we don't eat in just any old way what is put before us? And why is nothing put before us without a certain amount of preparation? Hunger has to be very strong before we will fail to be concerned with the quality of our food and the symbolic dimensions of the context in which we eat it. The term *appetizing* does not refer in the first instance to the sense of taste but to that of sight and smell. It is preparation and presentation that awaken the desire to eat. And here is something strange: the *eyes* excite the *mouth,* but just as soon the *hand* destroys what the *eyes* have seen so that the *mouth* can be nourished. However, if the eyes had seen nothing of the beauty that pleased them, if smell had detected no aroma, the mouth perhaps would have refused to open. This simply means that it is human beings who are eating and that the meal, in so far as it is food, is situated within a very broad exchange between human beings and nature, and an exchange among human beings themselves. In this exchange beauty is queen. And if we turn now to the Eucharist, why would we want to celebrate it as if it were a snack grabbed in the middle of our work rather than as the evening meal *(cena)* at which, at the end of the day, we refresh ourselves with the simple and beautiful rite that lets us be human beings?

Aesthetic sensibility is itself social. Taste in cooking and presentation depends largely on education. There is a tradition of "usages" as well as "recipes." Even on the level of food, and perhaps first at this level, a person is born within a culture. In the same way that the throat learns particular inflections for a language (when in principle a newborn is capable of all accents and tones), so also the palate receives a selective orientation in its appreciation of food that inserts a culture into the fundamental reactions of the organism to food. What European, leaving for Asia or Africa, has not been a little apprehensive about the food that may be encountered? The FAO (Food and Agricultural Organization of the United Nations) has been criticized for conceiving the problem of feeding the world on the basis of the eating habits of a middle-class American of the East Coast of the United States. But it is not enough to feed the world by thinking in terms of calories. We must think in terms of humanity—and a diversified humanity at that. Americans are the first to know this in terms of themselves. The number of foreign and exotic restaurants in their large cities is a witness to this. These restaurants let them rediscover the foods of their ancestors who immigrated to the New World. More simply, they introduce a necessary break with the insipid neutrality of fast-food restaurants, which perhaps are the symbol of a humanity on the path to losing itself. By partaking in the infinite diversity of human styles by means of a specific cuisine in a specific context, we could undo this leveling of cultural differences, which is so dangerous precisely because it concerns us on the level of our most basic functions.

Community

Food prepared in common is also food eaten in common. Cooking is not a matter of an arbitrary association of technicians at the service of a distribution among individuals, but rather of a community, which is a community of work and of life, of preparation and of consumption. The rise of a "super-civilization" that brings about both the promotion and the atomization of the individual was necessary before we were to see the birth of canteens and self-service restaurants, anonymous organizations of work where quality and quantity are determined by the number and the class of isolated individuals who will have recourse to their services with no communication among themselves. (Yet, as we shall see, the mere fact of taking a meal in the same place and in proximity to others does create a kind of ephemeral community.) Perhaps one of the signs of the deterioration of a civilization would be that it becomes more and more common to take a meal alone in a fast-food restaurant or at one's place of work. Whatever the case may be, the normal place of a meal (and for the majority of people, the real place, at least once a day) is the family or any other community of life, that is, the *communitas vitae,* bringing about and supposing at the same time the *communitas victus.* The important point is that nourishing oneself be the sharing of a common food and not the taking together of individual food, even if it is necessary in any case that distribution be equitable among all persons.

The importance of the community for the meal and, conversely, of the meal for the community can be verified by any number of signs. In *The Elementary Structures of Kinship* Claude Lévi-Strauss has drawn our attention to the painful situation of the single person in a primitive society who risked dying of hunger after having lived in abjection. And we know that in so-called advanced societies, single persons have to make a certain effort to feed themselves well and to preserve a dignified order in their meals, "as if there were someone there." Likewise, it would be rather superficial to be surprised at the importance given in ancient monastic rules not only to food (and fasts) but also to the meals. One of the most serious sanctions for a monk is to be excluded from the common meal and made to take his food "alone and apart." By the same token, for the monk to exclude himself from the common meal or to arrive late is regarded as a serious fault.[8] It is as if the truth of food could never in any situation be separated from the human community or from the ritual that the community appropriates for itself.

Step-by-step we see taking shape a sort of reversal in our way of considering food. We began by looking at the individual appetite and the way in which eating satisfies the appetite of each. It now is clear that there is no such thing as individual eating, except in extremely exceptional circumstances. The personal is inscribed in the social. To say it this way is simply to generalize a fact that can be verified from the very beginning of existence, because our first intake of food is situated already within an organic social relationship: the mother gives the infant her breast and the infant knows the mother whose breast it takes. *A social relationship that includes the biological*—this frame is probably never lost on any level of society at which we care to look. Thus our analysis of the meal provides us with a vantage point from which we can appreciate the tension between personal and communal. If eating means concretely taking part in food that has been gathered, prepared, and presented in common, then this means that human beings find themselves as subjects and persons within a community. What in us is individual and unrepeatable is simultaneously linked to something else. To encounter oneself is also to encounter oneself as a member of a community with which one is engaged both passively and actively.

Inviting the Stranger

The analysis of the meal in relation to the need for nourishment reveals the human being as linked to the whole of nature, inserted in the world as a totality in continual metabolism. The analysis of the meal as the fruit of culture, on both the technical and aesthetic levels, reveals the human being as linked to a community and not subsisting apart from it. It is through the mediation of the community that the relation of the human being to nature is realized, because from birth material nature is presented in a context defined by the reciprocity of persons. The mother and the infant—this figure always remains.

We can now take a further step forward if we consider another phenomenon, as mysterious as it is common: the invitation of a stranger to a meal. It is fairly easy to understand that a meal is taken in common among the members of a community founded on blood ties or on the same interests or work. But why is it that the table of this community is opened to someone who is not a part of it? Why is it that the stranger is invited into a world that is not his own? "Come some evening to dinner." But why?

In fact, is this so strange? If food and drink are the basic elements for human life and if these are consumed within a family or community of work, then doesn't the invitation to dinner signify that the stranger has become one of us? The food that we cannot do without even for a day in order to subsist—today we shall give it to the stranger. We shall give from our own subsistence, from our own foods, from our own life, in order that the stranger may live from it. To invite to dinner is, in the final analysis, to offer life. Sometimes the invitation precedes intimacy, but its intention cannot but become clearer: we want to establish a relation, and this desire is signified at the level that involves the whole person. The primacy of the body—this renders the invitation more alive and pressing. And accepting requires much.

WARDING OFF HOSTILITY

Can we take this perspective still further? It is necessary first to nuance it and to reduce to some extent its qualitative density, at least initially. Perhaps the invitation that seeks to establish a communion is in fact in many cases an attempt to disarm a hostility that is already present or may only be threatening. Or it is attempting to effect a reconciliation, to ward off a solitude, in short to put death at a distance and to insure one's own life rather than actually to offer it as gift to the other.[9] From group to group, from one person to another, there is no neutral relationship, no completely equal communication. Aggression or alliance are the only terms possible. This is certainly the case when food becomes scarce! On this level the offering very often becomes a defensive measure. Better to give and have less than to die. In this perspective the invitation to a meal, peaceful in itself, tends to establish an alliance on another plane, where in fact war and death may be threatening. What are "business meals" if not the expectant preliminary moves that have a contract in view that will allow the enterprise (and hopefully also its workers) to continue to live? If the contract is not concluded, the manifestations of ill will, deception, hostility, finally of "mourning," can quickly reveal that the invitation to life was not in reality addressed to the other but to oneself, yet through the other who was, by the contract, capable of procuring this life. Here the invitation to a meal would be a privileged sign of that subtle and measured play of exchanges thanks to which each person or each group preserves its own life. From Mauss and Lévi-Strauss we know that there are many other such signs of exchange: products, precious objects, even words, and finally—considered only on the level of their role in the survival of the group— women. It is quite possible that we live a good deal of the time at this level, but this is not necessarily without value. The test for discerning our intentions is easy: if we invite a friend or a couple to dinner a number of times and the "courtesy is never repaid," we will eventually stop. The proposed alliance will be replaced by a well-deserved hostility that will not fail to be exposed in conversations with third parties. We'll find unflattering names for the one who never returns the invitations always so readily accepted. This kind of person breaks the implicit rules of the game, which require that gift be answered with gift.

THE RISK OF EXCHANGE

The reason why we are examining here the possible breakdown of the mechanism of gift and counter-gift is to deepen our understanding of the whole phenomenon. The gospel in fact explicitly invites us to make a rule of such a possibility: "When you hold a lunch or dinner, do not invite your friends or your brothers or your relatives or your wealthy neighbors, in case they may invite you back and you have repayment" (Luke 14:12). Even without going that far, the risk attached to every invitation is clear. Why would someone accept it?

The rhythm of reciprocity by which two parties mutually give life to each other is in fact not possible except within the framework of a risk or the atmosphere of a drama, even if the success of an exchange may veil the tragic aspect. Exchange is the result of a game of initiatives. In order to begin, someone must risk a move: "Come to dinner this evening." Let us imagine such a phrase uttered not in our society of plenty but in a concentration camp, or more simply, in a place of poverty or a time of want. "Come, let's share." Here the one inviting is risking his own life in offering a part of what he has. Will the other, in a different occasion, do the same?

To invite is to place myself in a situation of inequality with the other, to design an asymmetric relationship. My own life is exposed in giving it away under the form of the food at my disposal. What might the outcome be? But the inequality here is just as quickly reversed. If, in offering, I submit myself to another who is going to be able to do what he wants with what I offer—this means to do what he wants with me!—the risk of accepting is no less great, especially if one is not in a position to return the favor. To accept is to recognize that the other is greater than me, that the other gives me life. I am reminded here of one of the heroes of Eugène Labiche, Monsieur Perrichon. Among the two suitors of his daughter, he prefers the one whose life he thinks he has saved over the one to whom he most certainly owes his life. Precisely because he owed this man his life, he was very near to hating him. The risk of losing myself is the same whether it is a question of giving or of receiving. Reciprocity is never just a simple game of harmoniously realized equilibrium. It is like a still point in the midst of a mine field: alliance at the heart of aggressions.

For the exchange to be realized in truth and not merely in appearance requires in some way a sacrifice in advance: either to give without hope of return or to accept without reservations. The wealth of the communication supposes for each side the "soul of the poor." As I have already mentioned, the gospel gives us two teachings. If it is a question of a meal, preference should be given to those who cannot repay. If it is a question of being invited, those invited should know how to free themselves from their affairs and interests in order simply to accept and to come (Matt 22:2–10). It is the law of "The one who loses gains."

EXCHANGE: THE UNIVERSAL HUMAN LAW

However simple and smooth it may be, this practice of invitation to a meal lets us perceive the human paradox: to give what we have and to be open to those who are lacking, wealth that is abundant and is given away, poverty that cries out and receives. The existence of these two extremes is the condition for that communication in which nothing is held back and all is given.

Other images come to mind that play off the image of the meal and that lead to the same reality. First, the image of conjugal love. Man and woman are each rich in their own sex but poor in the sex of the other. For them to attain the truth of their creation—"God created man in his image... male and female he created them" (Gen 1:27)—a communication is necessary between them, based on the mutual decision to give all and to receive all, no matter how difficult learning the art of love may be. This is the path of tender encounter, pleasure, indeed, the path of life.

Then there is the image of death as final gift. "No one has greater love than this, to lay down one's life for one's friends" (John 15:13). But here the mystery is more opaque. It is not easy to see immediately how reciprocity and communication are really established, because the one who has died, even if for the sake of love, has disappeared from the horizon of the living. I will attempt to clarify this later,[10] but any such attempt will always fall short of what we perceive intuitively and of what I said above: namely, that for the exchange to be truly established, it is paradoxically necessary to renounce all and to give, without counting the cost, all that one has. Who knows if death might not be the locus of a total alliance between gift and loss? We find here again the theme of sharing food in time of famine or water in the desert. The ease with which hospitality is practiced in regions less blessed with abundance perhaps suggests how deep within us runs the desire to make a gift of ourselves. Self-offering is a privileged place where one can truly achieve full humanity. Who knows if all our theology is not some kind of painful reeducation for people who have forgotten the basic laws of the art of living? It is as if all our plenty has made us lose view of the one rhythm that saves: gift and acceptance! A sole reality is in play, is gleaned, is amplified by means of all the great symbols from which our existence is woven: to procure food and simply to accept it; with tender caress to give the seed and to receive it; to let one's blood flow and to give our life so that another may live. With variations of intensity, this is the unique movement of life that shows itself and is realized.

Theologians have sometimes asked themselves if the Eucharist is a meal or a sacrifice, or else, how it can be both. But isn't this a false question whose point of departure is a narrow view of reality? To set the two in opposition is to see in a meal only the crude reality of eating, cut off from its symbolic connotations; and it is to see in sacrifice only a bloody oblation. But the Eucharist is a meal offered and accepted. It is substance given for the life of those who eat and life received with thanksgiving. And is the cross something other than this? As for the conjugal metaphor, it occurs again and again in liturgical texts. What is realized, then, at the table and at the altar, if not the encounter between the spouse and the bride as sung in the Song of Songs? The table is the altar, and the altar is the table because the one and the other are the mystical bed.

RESPONSIBILITY

Death for the sake of love is rare, and the cross of Christ is unique. The conjugal relationship is intimate and is lived privately only between the couple. The invitation to a meal, by contrast, is common and in the open. It is thus the clearest symbol of the deepest reality of the human person. Levinas proposes naming this reality "responsibility," but in its radical sense, before any ethical sense intervenes.[11] The human being *is* responsibility in a twofold sense. On the one hand, each person is responsible for any and all. Could it be otherwise since in fact all are taught to open their table and their house to whatever stranger should appear? On the other hand, all are responsible for the stranger—the stranger and the beggar who accepts every invitation without false pride. If we descend into the depths of ourselves, we will see that this is so. The invitation to a meal shows us what is true of every life: everyone is always in the position of being both host and guest, both simultaneously and successively. People who only always give are dangerously inhuman, and those who only receive are insignificant. Instead, the play between gift and reception creates a circulation of life in which and by which all find their joy and their fulfillment. It is as if true life really consisted in giving away all that I have, all that I am, and living from what others in their turn give me. Exchange, responsibility, love.

FIGURES OF DESIRE

Above, I suggested working with a conception of the human being in which brain, mouth, and hand would all be reconciled. This kind of humanism, however, would still lack something. It is doubtful whether such a reconciliation would be possible if we do not insert into the midst of these figures others more forceful than they: the right hand opened entirely outward and ready to give, together with the left hand turned within and entirely ready to receive; the sex of the man, which has its outward thrust but scarcely any sense of inward reception, together with that of the woman, who is reception and house but has no seed; and finally, the figure of blood, be it of man or of woman or of God, for it has always been understood without any need of explanation that "blood is life" (Lev 17:10–14).

We dream of a humanity in which these figures that symbolize the circulation of desire would triumph. The human being as worker, as artist, as an element of a material totality would remain, but would be penetrated by that true meaning, which creates a dynamic order in society and in the individual, as well as in the relations of each of these to the other. If the man of Marx "who produces his own means of existence" (with all that this entails) could one day recognize himself in the man of Levinas "who is responsible for all without previous engagement" (with all that this entails), then we would not be far from our goal! But for this to happen, it would be necessary perhaps to enter more deeply into the meaning of the symbols that I am trying to evoke here. I mean desire, which each symbol in its own way evokes. The total desire for communication and the desire for total communication—this is what would be seen in the reciprocal relation between all human groups, between all human persons, in which nobody possesses anything because everything is constantly being given and received. Such an all-embracing and dynamic community cannot in fact come from human beings by themselves. They must certainly receive it from the one from whom they receive this communal quality in their humanity and whose name they confess as "Father." The eucharistic symbol here would follow from the human symbol, transforming it.

But how can we be initiated into the truth of the eucharistic symbol if we no longer know how to invite one another to the earthly meal? Let us make every effort, then, to eat often one with another, neither in a shallow way nor with timidity. Then little by little we will understand just how broadly and deeply the exchange can extend.

Celebrating

The true meal is a feast. It is unfortunate that the word *feast* today evokes more the sense of the amount and quality of food than what the word means in its root sense. A feast is exceptional, a situation of social intensity, often connected to the strong moments of life or their memory. A meal is spontaneously a part of it because its symbolism unfolds in terms of the feast—birth, marriage, burial, inauguration, military victory. Whether in the family or in any group, it always involves events that concern life in its beginning, its transformation, or its end; and the celebrations gather the people who can participate in the joy or the pain that flows from these. It is not possible to see how a feast could be humanly complete if food and drink were not offered with a degree of liberality in direct relation to the importance of the event or the decisiveness of what it recalls. The invitation to a feast wants the other to share the joy or the pain, the significance and the influence of that which has happened or is being remembered. And those invited accept to enter into the game: the life of their hosts is more important than their fields or cattle or businesses. "Thank you for coming," we say as we say good-bye to our guests.

THE ANNIVERSARY MEAL

Let us take the simple example of an anniversary meal. It is essentially the evocation of life; and, if it is more than a habit or mere ritual, it communicates life and renews it. To celebrate in a family the anniversary of the marriage of an old couple is to recapitulate the wealth of their life together. It is to relive the birth of the children and grandchildren. It strengthens family ties that will then be expressed in a renewed way in other circumstances of life. It also purifies the negative aspects of the past and creates a new future.

When old soldiers celebrate the anniversary of a victory, it is to rediscover, at least in an ephemeral way, the strong bonds of a dangerous time shared together in the past. The meal receives from these memories an intensity of communication and meaning, which creates the feast. But at the same time it gives to these a sort of concrete reality precisely because there is a sharing of food that gives life. They are no longer sharing the wine of the trenches, but the wine shared today renews their sharing in the past and reestablishes their fraternity.

Thus, the anniversary meal is symbol and creator of life, provided, of course, that what is celebrated there reaches beyond the actual moment of celebrating the feast. If it does not spring from a sense of unity among those who have eaten together, it is no more than a mere ritual, empty of its human import and truth. From such as this derives the incomparable boredom of "official ceremonies." These are not real feasts because the people have not really given themselves away in them.

CONCERNING LANGUAGE

In the feast the value of total exchange connected to the invitation to a meal is thus redoubled and affirmed by the life celebrated in the event or memory that is the occasion of the feast. In the same way, the evocation of an impressive past overflows through the exchange of food and reveals its true meaning. Now I want to insert at this point, naturally and smoothly, a medium of communication that has been everywhere presupposed in what has been said so far but not examined as such: language. What could be surprising about this? The human person is that being who does not grab food from the ground with the mouth but who receives it in the hand from the hand of another. The mouth is free, not only to take in the gift received, but also to express thanks, to say words, to speak. And whoever gives food with the hand is the same one who utters the meaning of the offering with the lips. It is thus completely normal that the feast should imply language: by delivering the meaning, language is creator of communion.

At a certain moment of the celebration, during the meal or after it, speeches, toasts, and promises are *spoken* in order to share the reasons for the common joy. And it is to be hoped that a somewhat noisy support on the part of the hearers accompanies and approves the words that are said. In every meal words are exchanged at the same time as food. But the festive word is more than this spontaneous exchange. It reveals the meaning of this particular exchange of food; it speaks of the bonds that are hoped for or being celebrated; it evokes unity expressed in cries, noise, and acclamation.

Thus, gestures and things, events and memories all call for the word and render it fertile. The word, in its turn, uncovers and reveals the meaning of all of these. What might we say about this word?

Notes

1. This was said by G. Bachelard in 1938 in his *The Formation of the Scientific Mind*. Significantly, the phrase is taken from a chapter titled "The Myth of Digestion."

2. I discretely mention defecation here as a physical reality, included in the rhythm of eating, and the symbolic anal dimensions that are a part of it. I think, however, that if it is necessary not to

omit speaking of it (the gospel itself does, cf. Mk 7:14–23), it is also important not to center the analysis of food on it and to give it more importance than orality and its symbolic dimensions.

3. Slang also expresses the connection between symbols. Thus, food language expresses sexual relations since here also, even more so than with food, we intend an exchange of bodies that aims at a kind of infinity.

4. The pair nature/culture is perhaps like a founding mystery which it will never be possible to explain fully and whose terms cannot be isolated one from the other. Scholasticism spoke of a "real distinction" in reflecting on realities that were complex in their elements but unified in their origin. Something similar is the case here. I have reflected on this theme in my book *God, Time and Being*.

5. See M. Détienne and J. P. Vernant, *The Cuisine of Sacrifice among the Greeks*.

6. This phrase, "without separating or confusing" is borrowed from the Council of Chalcedon, where it is applied to the two natures of Christ (DS. 302). In fact, I think it is a heuristic and hermeneutical principle applicable to every domain of human knowing. It enables us to maintain a middle position between pretension and resignation.

7. *Mythologiques*, I. *Le Cru et le Cuit* (Paris, 1964).

8. *The Rule of St. Benedict* 24 and 44.

9. Evagrius Ponticus has said, "If your brother irritates you, invite him to dinner." *Ad Monachos* 15.

10. See chapter 4, section "Dying for Others," pp. 128–31.

11. This is a foundational theme in the work of Levinas. Probably we should nuance this, but to do so here would distract us from our present purposes.

CHAPTER TWO

Speaking

If food is a veritable epiphany of life, so too is the word, especially when it is addressed and exchanged in those moments of emotion and joy that we call the feast. The hand reaches out toward another and raises a glass of wine, the eyes open on the other's face, and from the mouth there comes forth a word of joy and remembrance. In the name of everyone, one of the participants addresses the hero of the feast, recalling a past and wishing a future. Such a discourse is *invocation*: the person of the hero is addressed with force and tenderness. It is also *evocation* because it is the remembering of a living past that has occasioned the feast and given the speech its *raison d'être*. This past is recounted—or more exactly, whatever from the past drew attention and elicited gratitude. Is such a discourse—invocation and evocation— just a fleeting rite, or does it actually carry life within itself? And who knows, does it contain something of eternity?

We will reflect now on its various aspects. Discourse is, first of all, voice; it is song; it is music. But it is voice for someone else, it addresses another and utters a proper name. Sometimes it is pronounced in the name of others. And so it begins to tell of something. Within an already established communion, it evokes, it remembers, and it also anticipates. In the end, it wants to become bolder and surpass the limits of time and space that are nevertheless the very conditions of its possibility. It wants to evoke origins, even the most remote, and to prophesy an end that will be an ultimate accomplishment. Will such talk end in failure? Or will it perhaps find in the invocation of God and the telling of his works the fulfillment it hopes for and which, ultimately, gives sense to every other word?

The Voice

A PERSONAL POETIC

There is neither invocation nor discourse if no one actually speaks. Once delivered, a speech can have the "honor of appearing in print." It can even be admitted that it had already been published or that the speaker had jotted down some notes beforehand. Yet whatever the importance of writing may be, the discourse, as language and invocation, does not *exist* except orally. It is the voice of an actual person.[1] The written text of a homily or the printed version of a televised interview can often be disappointing, precisely because the voice and its originality are missing. Of Christ it was said, "No one has ever spoken like this man has." Certainly this was because of the content of his message, but it was also very likely because of the seduction of his speech. Timbre, vocal preferences, articulation, movement, delivery, sonority—all these are individualized and are a sign of the person's self-expression. "I hear the voice of my beloved." For each person there is an oral rhythm, a personal manner of speaking, even if it is within an already perfected linguistic system. Choices (even unconscious ones), turns of phrase, images, particular words, the brevity or length of a phrase, the composition or imagination of a discourse—all this forms a sort of "personal poetic," irreducible to the content of the notions expressed, irreducible also to the universal genius of a language.

No language exists in the concrete except by means of this personal poetic, which reveals the person as much as it reveals what is said. Likewise, on the intelligible plane, it renders precise what is said. Certainly it would be possible today, more than in the past, to discover a number of universal structures at the heart of this personal poetic. In the same way that graphology lets us understand something of a personality through that person's writing, so also an "audio-psycho-phonology" could let us understand something of it on the level of the word (see Emmanuel Levinas, *Totality and Infinity*). But, in any case, this analytic step could not come except after the spoken word, and it remains to be proved if it could be exhaustive on all the planes of the oral personality. If language can be analyzed, it is because it is first given, because it has burst forth in invocation and discourse. What science could take account of such bursting forth? We know what art, what patience, what a sometimes interminable period of time is required to facilitate such bursting forth for the autistic child. Everything can be explained except the irreducibility of the spoken word, and all contents and all manners of reasoning depend on that irreducible word.

To speak is to form a musical phrase that is at one and the same time a sensual experience (visual, tactile) and a personal one (implying a unique reaction to what has been perceived). We could, by way of parable, offer a gloss on the word as it occurs in the primitive history of paradise. At the beginning of time, when God led the animals before the man so that he could name them, what did Adam do? With each one he sang a melody before God of his own invention that simultaneously produced and understood a sort of theme song of the animal being presented. This primitive song was at once *invocation* of God who had brought the animal and *evocation* of the animal brought. It expressed wonder or reticence, affection or fear. Later, when the man and the woman walk in the garden, the same modulations will be repeated. But from the moment when they were sung for the woman instead of directly for God, the inflection was slightly different. It was different again when the woman began to use them for the man, different once more when they sang together before God, different still when they sang them one to the other. The day arrived when the melodies became utilitarian, the necessary accompaniment for the budding techniques of raising foods. Or they formed stories to fill the hole left by an absence in time or space. It is in this way then, most likely, that from song the spoken word was progressively born, and from the poem, prose. Then there came the universals, knowledge, history, and science. A *universal* is that which is common to two interpretations of a same melody. To the extent that the music of language is understood and can be repeated, even with other tonalities and in other contexts, to other persons and by other persons, it is in part stripped of what made it something strictly personal and precisely situated. In this way the universal is born, which is extended yet further and plays in every key, from the level of common sense to that of sound. But none of this can be separated from the voice that at every moment takes it up and utters it again. To do so would be to make it something both dead and deadening.

The declensions in analytical languages like Latin and Greek testify in their own way to the desire preserved in language to be original and unique at every moment. The words want to be referred to the persons who are pronouncing them (the nominative), to the things they designate (the accusative), and to the person before whom they are pronounced (the vocative). Unless it is first evocative power of the mystery of existence, of development, and of communion, language cannot fulfill its unique mission of expression of homogenous domains that are recognized as such (universals, knowledge, history, science). Language is thus by essence multiform, even if this multiformity is manifested by the play of an activity of the senses that is always the same, inserted in a human time and place. Prose aspires to become the poem again, and the poem aspires to song. The language of knowing is interior to the language of evocation and invocation. The symbol, evocative and invocative, has primacy over the scientific symbol. Scientific symbol is not even possible except as relaying another symbol that embraces and includes it. And as for story and history, what is scientifically circumscribable is inscribed within that which it is not. The most refined interpretation of any content is like a preamble to (before) or a request for (after) the epic song itself, because the song is sung by someone to someone. The word addressed, common words surrounding the proper name, community created by the music and the evocation—where is all this spoken better and spoken more, where does one really come into contact with the death and resurrection of the Lord, if not in the thanksgiving of the eucharistic prayer? For here we have words sung to God our Father.

ADDRESS

Is it not because language is fundamentally an address that it is first music and that the spoken word is a song? And if voices are singing, they are singing for someone, for someone in particular. "Let me sing now of my friend the song of his love for his vineyard" (cf. Isa 5:1). That which the voice first expresses under melodic form is the beloved to whom it is addressed. The proper name is the little song in which like recognizes like, in its similarity and its difference. Can this be analyzed? The name is probably the most simple to analyze, but it is also the most important. "My dear Peter" or "My dear friend" or even "My dear boss"—always, implicitly or explicitly, this "my." It is as if it is not possible to speak to another without first making the other one's own, which in fact the other also must do to respond. To address the word is an act that creates unity and reciprocity. If the day should come when these are definitively broken, there will be no further talking. There is also always, implicitly or explicitly, a "dear." Such beginnings are characterized by emotion. Could I really address myself to another who had no value in my eyes? We can feel a particular silence as an expression of indifference or contempt. But the opposite is also true: each word addressed to us is a recognition. "Because you are precious in my eyes...and because I love you," God says (Isa 43:4). The religion of the *word* addressed could not but be a religion of *love* offered.

Then there are the differences: Peter, friend, boss.[2] A proper name, a relational name, the name of a function. It is always a person, but less and less intimately. If we give a party for the boss (the feast), it is because his leadership has been effective, his attitude just, his relations always correct and perhaps even warm. In the function a person is sketched: Peter. Paul, incompetent and uptight, could have quit the place with no one's regrets and with no feast. Yet because the proximity is so close, Peter also receives the name "friend" or its equivalent: dear friend, dear brother, dear cousin. Nonetheless, a sort of reserve remains that vanishes once the person is addressed by the proper name. In fact, this should not be done too soon. If people who first meet each other begin immediately calling one another by their proper names, thus immediately coming to a very personal designation, what names will they use when they truly know each other? At least let them not have the delusion that they know each other well just because they use first names and have foregone the long, slow approaches to others that forge real encounters. "Peter," in fact, is no longer a function or a network of relations. It is the man himself in the most absolute sense. "Peter" is what is called a proper name, that is, something incommunicable, which we wouldn't know how to use without a real closeness to the one we address in this way. It is as if there were no more intimate means to approach a person than by expressing what the person is in himself: irreducible, incommunicable, exclusive.

Can we push these reflections even further? A person does not really have a proper name until another has addressed that person with it. As a vocal or written sign the name, even the proper name, has a common and general significance. It could be the name "Peter" or part of the expression "peter out." There would be numerous people who would correspond to the name—all those who call themselves Peter, all those who call another Peter, all who will ever do so in the future. And a whole series of cross-references and precisions is necessary for the sign to assume its individual worth. "Peter, Son of Jonas." Or Peter Dupont, Peter Finn, Peter Whoever. But the real person, that person and no other, does not appear until the name is actually given him, until one addresses him: "Peter." Thus, the proper name is that which we *receive* here and now because someone has *given* it to us and we have heard it. Conversely, our proper name is that which we reveal of ourselves beyond the sign that, for better or worse, designates us. To call someone by name is to give being. Each time someone speaks to us, we are created. All that we will discuss in this chapter has its importance, but nothing is as important as the invocation of the name. In a certain sense we could say that a person who is never invoked really does not exist.

METAPHORS

In his *Totality and Infinity* Levinas uses beautiful metaphors to clarify this bursting forth of language. The word is like a face, he says, a countenance. A face is not something to be "stared at," a visible form upon which the eye fixes its grip. Rather, it is an icon that presents, reveals, and unveils itself in a freedom so radical that it precedes responsibility. It matters what we do with our eyes. We know very well how delicate it can be to look at another or to be looked at. The countenance is the very reality of the person who exposes and proposes herself. Yet it would never be possible to reduce the person to such manifestations or to pretend to control them. It is the same with the word: it does not completely exist until it has been received, and yet what is received is never exhausted.

There is also the metaphor of height (see *Totality and Infinity*). Every revelation comes "from above." A manifestation never takes place on an even plane; otherwise the originality of what is similar could be reduced to the already known. No, a manifestation comes from above and preserves a character of exteriority and difference that makes it attractive and mysterious. If the epiphany of a countenance and the sound of a word had not drawn me out of myself, so that I gently lift my eyes and attentively open my ears, would I ever have seen or heard anything other than the deceptive shadows and echoes of myself?

In the end, says Levinas, every spoken word is a teaching: not in the sense of a magisterially delivered doctrinal content but simply because, even if I already know what someone is going to say to me, I still have not heard the one who wants to say it to me now, and I do not know how what I think I already know will resonate within me. "If anyone supposes he knows something, he does not yet know as he ought to know" (1 Cor 8:2). So I must become a pupil again. The original way in which a truth is presented to us is part of the truth itself. This way, whatever it be, does not constitute a supplementary truth or another notion to add to a content. Rather, it is the living context in which every true discourse is inscribed. Truth does not exist except in the act of receiving, and as soon as I think I possess it, it slips away.

WHO SPEAKS?

All that I have said so far presupposes that the word is conscious and life occurs in exchange. But it could justifiably be objected that this is far from being everywhere and always the case. The word does not always burst forth—perhaps not even often—in the "first person." "One" says "what" one has to say, polemically and with an unconscious effort to justify oneself. The true "I," personal and free, does not appear in such a word. And so, someone is speaking to nobody, or at least not to the person in front of him, who is ignored and, in fact, not seen. If on the part of one or the other person the word remains in this impersonal category, its very content risks being falsified. The sentence becomes a defense, the story becomes contrived, and the reasoning fore-shortened.

Sick Language

We live, it is true, in a world where the word is sick. This has been the case for a long time. The work of Plato began under the banner of the impossible search for true language against the falsification of the Sophists. Every epoch flounders over the question of truth. Since Freud, we know better that our expressed language dances on the uncertain ground of a second, hidden language that lacks a true interlocutor. Yet I think that this in fact simply confirms the extent to which we desire a true language, a language where human beings can give life to one another by real (not false) address and real (not false) hearing, where symbols and concepts do not lack real references. Doesn't psychoanalysis attempt to reorient language toward the other—whether it be person or thing—and to unblock the mechanism that turns a word in on itself and in reality is really never spoken? We struggle so that our word may overcome the tendency to regress from the masculine, the feminine, or the plural to an impersonal neuter that comes from nowhere and is addressed to no one. This very struggle is evidence in favor of the word exchanged. Is it not also the foretaste of what one day will be an absolutely true word?

Difficult Language

It is true that sometimes it is necessary for language to develop a complex line of reasoning attached to some theoretical content difficult to expose, where the speaker concedes little to the ease of the listeners and where the listeners are so concentrated on grasping the content that they do not think about the person of the speaker. But this is more an indication of human weakness than a manifestation of the essence of language. Certain subjects are so difficult that it is scarcely possible for a speaker to pay attention simultaneously to them and to the persons to whom he is speaking. Sometimes this fragility of attention is temporary and needn't last any longer than is necessary to grasp the thought. Afterwards, it will be necessary to return to the listeners in order to verify if they have understood the gist of what has been said to them. Then can come examples, but these will make no sense if the language has not been first and foremost "address."

Impossible Language

It is also true that the occult quality of language is sometimes nothing other than the inverse of the superhuman effort to say in words "that" which eludes all understanding and which always lies beyond all signs, even the most refined and elaborated. Human language is probably scarcely more than a limited guidepost along the path that comes from a place we don't know and leads to no definite place. To suggest this "beyond" of every origin and every end—this infinite that paradoxically allows the definite to be said—we do what we can! "On Mount Carmel there are no more paths." We try to go to the root of metaphors; we combine words that are opposites; we seek to attain the point where we sense that it is nonsense which has sense. In doing that we discover that something, perhaps someone, speaks to a place in us deeper than ourselves and mysteriously directs our language games toward an extreme where we ourselves could not have led them. To recognize that "that speaks" becomes for us a confession of humility. Our own language astonishes us. We do not know where the word we hear ourselves saying comes from. If then the hearer of such language grasps nothing of it, is it not because the hearer's ear lacks the one essential resonance? At the beginning and always there is the poem.

Analogical Language

The ultimate language is undoubtedly impossible and it can be approached through the poem. However, the one who is sometimes led to speak poetically, or rather who allows the poetic word to move interiorly, is also someone who speaks on other more modest levels, who uses other literary genres in which the intelligible address and content are more accessible. My conviction—and I realize that it is open to discussion and takes a particular line among the philosophies of language—is that we will never have a total resolution of the continuity between different levels of language. It is certainly more difficult to elaborate the connections and the analogies between different levels of language than it is to privilege an inaccessible mystical language. But this leaves ordinary talk that we don't hesitate to use elsewhere without any foundation. In the gospels there are different densities of the word, but there is always the man Christ who is expressing himself, and his discourse cannot be ignored because it is neither vulgar nor esoteric. Perhaps the reason is that Christ knew from what depths the word and his prayer rose up in him and to whom they were addressed. For us, at least, there remains this much: if we speak a language that seems to go to the very edge of its limits and seeks to surpass itself by employing its hidden resources to the ultimate degree, it is still necessary to ask ourselves to whom such language can be addressed and, if it comes from beyond ourselves, who it is that could listen to it. Does not the ultimate prowess of mystical language come to us from a God who invokes and to whom one can address oneself? And is not this the ultimate horizon of every word?

As a conclusion to all these questions, it could be said that in all our speaking, even in the best possible speaking, we remain in expectation of "true discourse": truly addressed in a live invocation, proceeding from a subject knowingly speaking from the depths of himself, having sound reasoning, stories with genuine meaning, liberating decisions. Can't the gospel, and even more concretely the eucharistic word, be envisaged here and now as the fulfillment of such an expectation?

Representation

There is yet another aspect of speaking that we need to consider. In certain circumstances the spoken word can be carried by one person in the name of all. The uniqueness of a speaker, and also of those in whose name the speaker speaks, would seem to preclude any possibility of representation. As for the listeners, if for them there is something unique in hearing their names invoked by a neighbor or friend, how could this invocation replace all others? Does the voice of the older son drown out all the others? Is it the voice of Esau or the voice of Jacob?

To represent is certainly not to replace. Nothing can substitute for the personal word, and no personal word can pretend to supplant others. In one sense the representative who speaks can only be herself. This can be verified by noticing that she will be personally thanked for her discourse. She will be praised for her choice of words, the way in which she expressed herself, the feeling with which she did so. She is not confused with those in the name of whom she speaks. Joy will be warmly expressed that it was she who was chosen to proffer the word. In this way, all that is uniquely her own seems actually to contribute to the quality of the representation rather than to impede it.

THE FIRSTBORN

We can look at some situations in which a person speaking in the name of others helps us to understand the dynamic of representation a little better. There is, to begin with, a sort of spontaneous primacy: the first in time has a kind of "natural" right to speak in the name of those who come after, for the first has been a pioneer. The firstborn speaks in the name of the brothers and sisters because, as first, he or she made parents of the man and woman who had the joy of bringing this first child into the world. After the first child, the pattern repeats itself; but the initial event, like all beginnings, had its own density that cannot be compared to what follows. The oldest disciple speaks in the name of the others because, as first, he made of the professor a master...Representation arises here from a sort of superiority of the initial event over any of its repetitions, even if the repetitions also have their own originality.

THE DEPUTY

Every person who speaks is also someone who listens. The listener receives the revelation of the other's countenance, submits to what manifests itself as coming "from above," and is instructed by this information. All the while remaining oneself, the listener is also enriched by contact with the other. When a community of the word is thus established, in a reciprocity that does not dissolve the persons but puts them in communion with one another, then, without replacing the others, one of its members can speak in their name, precisely because this one is able to reecho their accord. This is the most normal foundation for representation. It implies that the persons represented have accepted in some way or other that one of them should be heard in the name of all because all recognize themselves in the representative.

THE BEST

Finally, it can be imagined that in a group there is a person so complete and unique as to be able to recapitulate the other persons, all of whom are in principle capable of expressing and revealing themselves. In the manifestation of this countenance and this word, every countenance will be revealed, every person manifested and entirely recognized, even while knowing themselves surpassed by a quality that they have not attained. This happens in all groups, even if not all have the generosity to recognize it and pass the word to another. Does this point of view not raise the question of wanting to discover one who would be the best, not merely of a particular group but of the whole of humanity throughout the entire course of time and space? If there were someone who could speak in the name of all human beings, who might that be? And to whom would such a one speak? We see open before us here a path for knowing Jesus Christ, the human being who speaks to God in the name of all human beings.

If, then, the phenomenon of the word proffered manifests the uniqueness of the person who speaks at a level even deeper than the words said, the practice of representation indicates that the person, though unique, is not exclusive, not alone in the world. Persons cannot be interchanged, but they can be represented, unless everyone is a monad closed in on itself. Each person is at one and the same time *in* oneself and *for* others. The words said will be one's own, but in such a way that they can be uttered in the name of others and heard by others. And by these words *all* will be *one*, without ceasing to be themselves.

Evocation by Story

The content of a speech may be a story, that is, the evocation of a past that is to be celebrated. This evocation finishes in general with wishes that anticipate a bright future and prosperity *ad multos annos*. However, in order for the story truly to be what it ought to be—faithful and evocative—it must be preceded by the invocation of the one to whom the story is addressed. I can neither understand nor reveal what I refuse to be involved in. A certain emotion is required for my objectivity. If the past I evoke has not become mine, how can I say it? And since in a certain sense the past is not mine (I was not yet born, I was not there, I didn't know...), then it must become so. I must enter into community with those who have lived what I propose to recall to them. In addressing myself to them I lose the exteriority that prevents me from understanding. *Their* past through *my* language is taken up again in *our* present. And since all is not finished when the feast ends, we henceforth embark together toward the future, which in part awaits us and which in part we will make. The true story flows forth from an immense tact on the part of the one who recounts. It belongs to the speaker to "touch" what resonates with life and death. We know this well but perhaps only in negative fashion. "You can count on me not to 'touch' on that point." Touching intrudes much more in the saying than in the not saying. And so to avoid saying things poorly, it is necessary for the speaker to become identified by invoking those whose lives are going to be touched.

A not uncommon scenario can illustrate what I am saying here. The rules of etiquette can require that the privilege of giving a toast be confided to some honest and tedious old gentleman. He is endowed with a stubborn memory of years long past and, always indignant, he is ever ready to recount his own life and its projects under the pretext of evoking the past of the person to be feasted. His painstaking reconstruction and interminable recital are listened to politely by the adults, while the children start to become agitated. The sense is broken, the rhythm blocked.

To recount is not to say all that ever happened. Archives, history, and evocation should not be mixed up. Conversely, we well understand that such an evocation should not be fantasy. The events that make up someone's life should not be played with lightly. Nor is it proper to choose events and present them in such a way as to verify a preestablished thesis. The "moral of the story" or the anti-moral have no place here, but only the flow which signifies that a life has had its joys and its sorrows. Thus, to recount is to structure a discourse that avoids saying everything and fabricates nothing. It is to discern the real events that have marked a life. It is to perceive their interconnections. It is to present a meaning or sense that can be identified with a life. Every bit as much as in good fiction, the story does not allow for a word-for-word recounting. Poetry is what is required. When the insistence on "what actually happened" becomes too great, there is no longer a *story*. The dimension of language has been forgotten, as if we could do without the mediation of the recounting. Or, at the other extreme, when the "real" reference of the story is taken too lightly, then nothing is narrated. Language ceases to be mediation. It takes itself as its own end. It becomes fiction when it should have been evocation, or verbal process when it should have been Eucharist.

STORY AND INVOCATION

We could approach this from the opposite direction. There is a story within the speech of the feast. Generalizing, it could be said that every story deprived of its festive context calls for one and awaits it. Apart from this context it can only be provisional. In the end, it is always to someone else that a story is told, and this direction toward the other is the best guarantee of the truth of what will be said. Let us take some examples.

The Insignificant Story

First of all, there are insignificant stories that we tell and listen to. But even if insignificant, they are still important. Does a man come home from work in the evening or from a business trip without a surprise? He will speak briefly to his wife and spontaneously elicit from her a brief story. "Did you have a good day?" This exchange is normal. Silence would need explaining in this circumstance. It would be a sign of avoidance, disagreement, fatigue, or some other such thing. By reproducing orally the course of his day and by asking his wife for a similar word, the husband gives himself to her once again. Such stories are told on the foundation of an already existing communion, which itself has been sealed with a word. The stories reconstitute this communion, or at least maintain it. What matters here is less the content recounted than the exchange of the word itself. It is an ongoing expression of communion between persons. Too many details would not be appropriate here. To say or ask too much would be as abnormal as saying nothing at all.

The Importance of Events

Events themselves are not without their importance. If insignificant stories maintain communion, significant ones create it, reinforce it, or even give it a new direction. If I've just barely missed having an automobile accident, the first thing I'll do when I see a friend will be to tell about it, and the friend will share in my emotion. The reality of the accident no longer exists except in the telling, but there would be no telling without that reality. We can gauge the importance of the role that telling has by noticing that it is only while I am speaking to another of the danger barely missed that I take its measure. The emotion can reach a greater intensity than in the event itself. Thus the reconstruction of the event in the discourse becomes more real than the fact itself as it was experienced. Or, from the other direction, the hearer can relive the event recounted with greater intensity than the teller and so reveal the density and importance of what has happened to the one to whom it happened.

In the same way, it is very important to listen to a child tell the story of a day happily spent. The child relives it with force and tries to make others share her interests. If the other is listening only with a distracted ear, she insists. We have here once again confirmation of what I am arguing: the story emerges in the context of mutual invocation. Invocation creates the space for the exchange of words, and it effects a selection process of what—from among all the events available to memory, near and far—will be told now in this story. In any kind of group—familial, religious, or political—there are events that get classified as "We don't speak about that." Why? In the hope that silence here might be the prelude to forgetting? The memory and the sharing again of such events would only destroy the group and lay it waste.

On the other hand, we don't just recount *it-doesn't-matter-what* to *it-doesn't-matter-who*. To receive the communication of certain traditions is part of initiation into a group. There are certain stories that are not told "to others," to those outside the group. These examples show that this is not about withdrawing from others. Yet a pure neutrality does not exist. Truth needs a particular context in order to emerge and be received. This is why the more an event has had density, the more its telling is marked by historical veracity and the more it must strike people at the heart of their desire, provoking in them communion and the feast.

OF WHAT DO WE SPEAK?

Let us briefly consider the content of our stories. What do human beings tell about among themselves? What events do we speak about? I will not try here to establish an orderly and exhaustive nomenclature. I want, rather, simply to take account of our everyday conversations.

Nature

First of all, we speak of nature, more concretely, of good weather and bad, rain and sun. Like everything that is common and familiar, this reflex is full of significance. It is a kind of admission of our radical dependence, even if it can also be a means of limiting communication. Every conversation supposes this milieu of day and night, of rain and sun that is common to us all and to which everyone is sensitive. So, naturally, we speak about it. And if someone speaks only of the weather, it is probably because there is a desire to avoid talking about anything else—unless, of course, there is big, disturbing weather or some other major natural event, like a prolonged drought, an avalanche, or an earthquake. In any case and no matter at what level weather is discussed, what we say about rain and sun and all the rest establishes, without our realizing it, a cosmic base. Sun and water on the earth and on our bodies, but also drought and storms and cyclones—this is the context for the stories human beings tell.

Ruptures

Next, we speak about ourselves. I mentioned above the importance of the insignificant story. When there is a story to tell, however, it is usually not the everyday, but the exceptional, that inspires it. By "exceptional" I mean whatever inscribes a difference onto the ordinary fabric of our rhythms, habits, efforts, and encounters. This inscribing might be in the *body*: we tell of accidents or sicknesses, and this in the perspective of death—death warded off, death dreaded, or perhaps death accepted. Or the inscribing could be in *space*:

we tell of movements, arrivals, departures. Or in *relations:* we tell of encounters that move between the poles of communion or conflict, love or war, and the consequences these entail. Or in *work:* we tell of discoveries or we display a masterpiece. All these things and many others like them have in common that they stand out from more neutral everyday things and have interrupted their monotonous course. In one way or another the individual or the group has had to react, decide, and choose. An awareness and a word has been taken up and set in motion by the passions. Directions have been freely chosen.

The story brings to life again that mix between the tangle of circumstances that are, in part, independent of our influence, and those mysterious moments when someone's inner strength of will imposes itself on these circumstances and bends them in a different direction. Without that intervention what happened would have been only the unfolding of a blind logic. The story gives us back this tangle of forces, but henceforth in the form of a "model" or "pattern." It brings to the fore and preserves for the memory that strange mixture of imperative necessity and unexpected adventure out of which every significant event is composed. It takes up again and develops the line of power and influence that this event opened. Yet—and here we see it again—the story is not possible except within the perspective of communion and participation, and its objective truth depends on the greater or lesser capacities of the teller and the hearers to employ those mysterious forces whereby human beings give form to an event.

It can sometimes be said of a historian that his narration is "materially exact" but that "he hasn't understood anything of what he is talking about." To tell the truth, there is no single comprehension of a fact, simply because the protagonists themselves have contributed to it in different and even contradictory ways. In recent years there have been best-selling books on such events as the creation of famous Renaissance artworks and the American Revolution. Would it ever be possible to have a single narration of these events? This is obviously impossible. We will have to wait for the end of history to grasp in its total truth the reality and impact of any single event.

Faith

The requirement of communion and participation intrinsic to the story is found again if we observe the phenomenon of the response that is made to it, most clearly seen in the *reaction* of the hearer. The word *faith* is useful here. It implies, first, a certain trust, a recognition of the generosity of the one who really wants to tell us what has happened or who wants to share with us what is known of it. It is also a recognition of being invoked, which becomes invocation in return, translated into attention. In faith there is likewise an element that concerns content. What is told to me is true, it really happened, it produced the series of consequences that I am hearing about. I am engaged not only with the person who speaks but also with the content told. This gives rise to a language of adhesion, a sort of implicit repetition of the story. To say "yes," "right!," "amen" is not to give a word-for-word repetition but rather its short equivalent. It is going ahead of the truth of another and receiving it as one's own. And if from the story that is told some concrete engagement results for the teller, that engagement should also become mine. I am "com-promised" when I choose to hear and to believe what is told me. After that, can I wiggle out of what must follow next?

For there is always a "next." If a story is told to create communion, then a future is born from this communion. If we recall among ourselves the memory of the past we have made, if we have faith in one another, is it not so that we can better construct our future in connection with what we have been and what we are? The recollection of the past makes no sense unless it is joined to an anticipation and a projection of the future. Otherwise it would be nothing other than sterile repetition, a nostalgic memory that would alienate us from our present and all its possibilities. Telling the story of what we remember is an expression of desire and hope.

So what has finally happened during this evening when we found ourselves together to celebrate a golden or silver jubilee? In the feast we have repeated a process of exchange that has marked the long period that we wanted to commemorate. Some people did the inviting to the meal; others brought gifts. The means of life were thus exchanged and then shared. A communion of material things—of bodies—revealed that the people themselves were completely involved with one another; they were exchanging themselves with each other. Hands were shaken; there were embraces, laughter, and tears. In this *present* moment of the feast, the word arrived to take hold of the commemorated *past*, to recognize it, exorcise it, give thanks for it, and to direct it toward a *future* of communion. It has not been a question of reconstructing every detail of the past, nor of painting it in colors more or less lively than the way it was. The story as told during the feast forgets a great deal, and this is normal. It is silent about much, and this too is normal. Such silence is mutual pardon, a conjuring away of what was not life. But, through all the joys and trials, the story does tell of the life that has been given, received, and passed on. The very doing of this opens time.

The Word Beyond Its Limits

DEATH

A festive jubilee opens time because it celebrates life. It cannot conjure death away, however. I mean the death of those being feasted, who are closer to their end than their beginning. I mean the death of the institution, which cannot always survive in the way it has done. I mean the death of a significant event, because memory gradually falls away from it. And so the question is posed: Should we simply admit to our powerlessness to conjure away death and be content to opt for life during the short span given us? Or is death, instead, an event whose memory we would *never* know how to erase and, consequently, for which human beings will *never* be without words, food, and drink? Would its feast then be permanent? And such an event—who would be able to evoke it? Addressing whom?

TO SAY BEGINNINGS

We spontaneously think of "the beginning," that mysterious period we designate in a plural that is equally mysterious: "origins." This primordial moment is in effect what all people tell about, concerning which all cultures offer stories, modulated along all the registers where the human word has ever ventured to reach. In returning to "the beginning," do we not reach the limit point common to all human beings and concerning which all peoples exchange memory in a universal feast? I mean the feast that grips the human being at the very roots, consequentially engaging the whole of humanity along its true path and aiming at a future as absolute as "the beginning."

The Passion for Origins, the Passion for Oneself

In any case, this "beginning" interests us. No matter by what path it is approached, it unceasingly holds our attention. And we are not without intelligent popularizations that put the average person in touch with the current state of research. The interest in paleontology and what it conjectures about human origins never slackens. Upstream from that is the ever present passion for the beginnings of the universe as investigated in the disciplines of astrophysics. The "history of time" is an enigma concerning which we continue to search out the mystery. Then there is the heritage of Darwin or the speculations of Einstein or Max Planck. Schelling's philosophy of mythology has become popular again, not to mention the more phenomenological approaches of Eliade or the structuralist approaches of Lévi-Strauss. Some decades ago myth regained its rightful place, and its importance and significance in a contemporary understanding of the human situation is recognized everywhere. And finally, if we turn to the Hebrew and Christian scriptures, are there any passages more closely examined than those in the first chapters of Genesis?

All this seems to show that the passion that urges human beings to reach back to their origins is universal. It is more fundamental than the irreducible diversity of approaches. It is as if all these different approaches were nothing other than multiple garments for a single passion. It is as if memory wanted to return as far up and as far back as possible, all the way to the point where there would be nothing more to remember because there is nothing to remember. The passion for the beginning precedes and sets in motion all the approaches toward it.

But what in reality is this passion for origins if not a passion for oneself and a concern for one's future? Before thinking about the origins of the world, every person thinks of his own origins and poses the question of his birth. Where do little babies come from? How did I come into the world? We must enter into this question a little more deeply.

What actually are we asking? Why, instead of posing the question of our own origin, don't we just live in the present with the memory of an immediate past? Wouldn't that be sufficient to orient us toward a stable future? Or let us grant that it is necessary to go back to infancy in order to comprehend completely our mature age. But what is the sense of the question about the first moment of our birth, of which we could certainly not reconstruct the experience? It is because the question of birth does nothing other than transcribe, in question form, a radical restlessness. People searching for their roots confess that they cannot do without them. We trace our way back to an original point—first by memory, as far as it leads, then by questioning. This is an attempt to conjure away a dangerous fragility and to establish a safe framework where one is not "too much" cast into the world without relations or dwelling. No, on the contrary, I am born of this man and that woman. I have a proper name that does not designate me except by relating me to others. I am "Michael, son of Peter and Nicole," a member of this family from which I can venture out to other people and to the world. How can I build a future if I have no past?

A Response in the Form of a Story

Where will the answer to this question about the beginning come from? For after all, we cannot reconstruct the experience of our birth, and its origin lies too deep within us for us to have any memory of it. The answer can only come in the form of a story. Someone else must tell me who conceived me and where I was born. I am thus placed in the position of having to believe the word that gives me the answer, and I cannot really completely verify it. So the anguish of my native fragility does not disappear. And it will not disappear by means of a who-knows-what that would transform it into proud assurance, as if at last I had experienced by myself that *I am*—born of myself, here today out of my own being and my own certitude. No, such anguish does not disappear. Yet it is somehow overcome when I believe the story that is told me of my birth. I accept giving the names of father and mother to those who tell me that I am their child. In this way I accept being dependent on my origins and limited in my being, and yet I also get around this limitation by locating myself within a line of offspring and in a place. Doing this, I arrive at what I cannot draw out of my own self: the truth of my mysterious concrete nature is liberated by my consenting to the birth I have received and to the name that was given me.[3]

The story of my birth reveals something similar to what I already discussed concerning the mystery of a proper name. I said at the beginning of this chapter that I have no proper name until someone gives it to me. And further, if I have a name, it is because someone calls me. There is an old Breton riddle that goes like this: "What do you have that is yours and which is no use to you but is useful to me and others?" Answer: my name! For the name was given to me, and it is mine. With it I am at the disposition of others so that they can call me. It is only in being-at-the-service-of that I find myself. We have arrived again at Levinas and his definition of the human being as responsibility: to respond is to be; to believe is to exist. The joy of birthdays is thus the sign of my having consented, the feast that reintegrates me into my relationships and into my space, thanks to the memory of my birth, rendered present in the story of my origins and in the name I carry. It is also the story of my hope, an opening onto time ever moving forward.

THE WORD ABOUT ORIGINS

The general question about origins gives ultimate and universal form to the more limited question about my birth. I am "Michael, son of Peter and Nicole." But who is Peter? Who is Nicole? The father and mother are not more absolute than the son, and the assurance provided by the revelation of being their son is still too partial, just as is the risk of accepting it. The son is also a brother; the brother is also a cousin. There are lateral relationships, but extending how far? There are ancestors and descendants, but extending how long? There are friends and companions, groups both friendly and hostile, extending from one point to another all the way to the ends of the earth. With each individual life is related, and without these bonds, that life has no sense. The stories that concern me or my group are only a small part of all that is told among human beings. The universal memory of humanity is the full horizon against which every far-reaching personal or collective memory is told.

But if this is how things are, can a person live and die—that is, cover one segment of time and evolve in a particular portion of space—without hearing a word about the beginning and perhaps also about the end, without hearing a word about the inhabited world and all the rest of the cosmos? Or is it perhaps not really necessary to reach all the way back to the very beginning, moving backwards from one fragment of history to another? And as for the future, is it perhaps not enough just to engage oneself for the short run, without wondering about the eventual outcome of the sum total of human activity?

Today there are any number of efforts to construct a scientific account of origins, and these are articulated implicitly or explicitly, in greater or lesser degrees, in coordination with some form of envisioning the end. In other cultures mythic representations are most certainly concentrated on recounting origins. This is enough to convince me that the human person will never be satisfied to live only from a partial and limited memory, or only from a limited anticipation of the future. Nonetheless, we can ask if science and myth successfully answer this lurking question about origins and about the end. Do these really tell us what gives us our name—"human being"—and do they tell us to whom we can respond?

The Scientific Story

The scientific representation is in fact anthropocentric. And yet, the question of the beginning expresses an unformulated, half-conscious conviction felt by everyone: I am not the center. Modern science has displaced this anthropocentrism somewhat; but it has not erased it. It is true that Earth is but a modest planet circling a sun of medium grandeur. Yet it is still true that it is from this Earth that human beings have discovered the plurality of worlds, none of which, up to the present, has proved itself capable of engendering life, not to mention the spirit. The generous hypothesis that there may be other inhabited worlds does not alter our present ability to understand the mechanisms of the cosmos and so to control them to a certain measure. It is likewise true that humans are neither the first living things nor the first animals to appear on Earth. Even so, it still must be admitted that all the theories of evolution are anthropocentric. The flow of the development of life has gone toward the human. We cannot think of life except in relation to ourselves. The enormous changes that the Copernican and Darwinian revolutions have brought to our images of world and people have still not displaced the theme of human being. If humans are not the center, they are at least a point of reference for the real. In this sense the sciences remain inside what could be called the anthropological circle, and they do not answer the essential quest for an "elsewhere" (both upstream and downstream in time) with reference to which we could situate ourselves. The sign of science's failure in this regard is that the scientific story does not give rise to any feast. Learned paleontologists will joyfully celebrate the birthdays of their children, but it would not occur to them to promote a "Birthday Party for the Human Race." Similarly, the astrophysicist would not know how to think about the Big Bang or any other theory of an "absolute beginning" as a reason to celebrate a feast. As for the end, the picture painted by science is not pretty: everything ices over completely and then the black hole. In science's scheme everything happens as if in the "beginning" there was no one there to give a name to what was born, and at the "end" everything will simply disappear. The gap between an individual birth that is significant in the framework of a family or a people and the collective silence about the mystery of origins is enough to indicate the insufficiency of the anthropocentric scientific explanation. This explanation is clearly of some use, but it must necessarily be included within a larger vision. And so we arrive again at something already said above: when it comes to story and history, scientific discourse is interior to what is not science. But where can this other truly fundamental discourse be found?

The Mythic Story

By contrast, the mythic representation unfolds largely around beginnings conceived as birth. It does so within the context of a liturgy that often commemorates together the enthronement of the *king* (the human being), the beginning of the *new year* (time), and the appearance of the *world* (space). Thus it recounts a more or less imagined history of the origins of the Earth and what fills it, as well as of the human beings who find their dwelling there. However, this history is told in a nostalgic way. It seeks to take account of the origin of evil and death as much as, if not more than, the origin of the Earth and of human beings. The myth recounts more the beginning of death than the beginning of life. It tries to reach beyond this human birth now marked by death and to arrive at the time and space—unknown, but imagined and desired—where beatitude and immortality reign. Here the feasts that celebrate these myths evoke and recreate, unless they are celebrations of mourning for those sacred times long since vanished and for those dead heroes, the likes of which we will never see again. In this way the myth inserts living human beings into the closed and flawless network of an essentially regressive ritual law and social practice. This ritual and these practices define collective behaviors capable of establishing a certain communication between the world of origins and the present world, from which it is necessary to conjure away the death that has marked it at its core. The myth of origins forbids in principle every opening or innovation. So it is not a myth of birth, even if it recounts at length a history of the first appearances of nature and of life. Rather, it is more a myth of *before* birth that wants to overtake human beings who are now *after* death. Thus, the authentic myth of origins cannot be situated in the *once upon a time* and the *beautiful deserted island*[4] in which the mythic story creates an ideal space (devoid of every tension and every future), an ideal space of which our present world would be only the degradation.

Word and Feast of Creation

If the scientific description and the mythic story do not successfully respond to the question of origins, what language does? The answer is clear. In the same way that the story of his or her birth is critical for each individual, so the story of its origins is for the whole human race. I said it above: when it is a question of birth or of death, neither memory nor anticipation of the event is possible. These require a word coming from tradition with a feast that seals its truth. I was born and I can say so because I have received a name; I carry it, and others celebrate it with me. Now, isn't the question of origins something like the question of an *ultimate name*? I don't mean the name given to one person by another, for this always retains a certain exteriority. Rather, I mean the name that reaches every human person at the core of each one's humanity, in a singularity that constitutes every sign and reaches the whole of the human race. If my parents teach me (in Levinas' sense that every word is a teaching) that I was born, and if the life of other human beings makes me learn that I must die, and if I can speak of my birth and death in the faith that is acceptance of these fundamental traditions that concern me, then who can tell the human race of its primordial birth? And if it is a question of death, to whom can one entrust one's life? Would it not be the one who not merely gave birth to that person, as his parents did, but the one who created him and all the world that sustains him? And what could the language of origins and of the end be if not the response of thanksgiving to this revelation of the gift of being and of life, in a hope stronger than death?

We could say the same thing coming from the other side of the story. To whom can a person tell her beginnings? To whom can she express her hope for the future? Who is the other to whom her story is addressed? For we have said that every story is an exchange. Obviously, to a certain extent it is simply to other human beings that one can speak of origins and of the end. Such speech is a mutual exchange on the mystery of destiny. But another human being could not be an adequate hearer of the story that bears the whole of humanity and the entire world. How could one person completely hear the story that so fully engulfs the one telling? In so far as it concerns the genesis and the end of a world, the only one with whom these events can be spoken about and exchanged is the one by whom this world came into existence and by whom it is led to its end. This is the one whose person and whose reality are expressed for us in the activity of creation and its fulfillment that we try to tell about and evoke. In other words, the proper place for the evocation of origins and the end is the religious feast. Here story finds its ultimate dimension, for it is story *addressed*. It is celebration of God the creator, and the story of creation unfolds *within* the celebration. It is also acknowledgment of God as savior. It stands in sharp contrast to the mythic story which, by its search for an impossible purity of history, blocks the origin of being and the origin of evil. Instead, the feast that truly liberates us must evoke time in a way that really "says time," in a way that repairs its huge wound and opens it continuously toward a fulfillment capable of awakening desire.

In the perspective that I am trying to sketch out here, God does not enter on the scene primarily as the "cause" without which nothing of what is recounted could have existed or could continue to exist. Even if God is that, to see him only under this aspect would be to include him within the story as its point of departure: "God as one of the elements of the story." In reality, God is the other before whom the story is told. God is the one to whom human beings address themselves when it is a question of creation and salvation, for God alone can respond to this story. Furthermore, we would not be able to tell this story had God himself not first given us the name that is identical to being and to history through which we can address ourselves to him. God alone, the one who made Heaven and Earth and every living thing on it, the one who addresses human beings in the words of a covenant, God alone can be so invoked in a spirit of exchange and communion—if it is true that the very essence of story implies invocation and that story exists through invocation. The historians of religion tell us that in the mythic narratives the unique God and creator scarcely appears. He is rather the idle God, *Deus otiosus.*[5] People addressed themselves rather to gods and to demons, to spirits of every kind, seeking to conjure their influence or ensure their protection. Such myths and their corresponding feasts do not establish this universe of true language between gods and human beings. St. Augustine already observed this in *The City of God.*[6] This observation can help us to delineate "true religion." True religion listens to the one God. This God speaks. (But where and when?) True religion responds to God in the feast and in rendering thanks for the beginning and the end, for the covenant and the promise. (But where is this feast celebrated and who celebrates it?)

The Poem of True Origins

What am I proposing here if not the very limits of the story that *is* invocation? When the story is at the limits because it treats of the beginning, then invocation is response and thanksgiving. I cannot comprehend myself in my first coming forth unless I accept the gift I have received, the gift that causes me to say "my Father" to the one who gives it to me. And humanity cannot really comprehend itself in its origins except in reference to the one by whom it exists. In doing so it discovers itself to be entirely "posited" by the one who has given it its name. Now humanity says in response, "Our Father." What really can set us free for true life? Would it not be our acceptance of our finitude and our allowing death to enter the periphery of our vision? But I don't mean merely a resigned acceptance. What sets us free for true life is accepting what we are and, at the same time, inserting its language into a trajectory that surpasses it.

Situated inside this invocation of God, the story of origins will not be totally homogeneous with our other stories, nor will it be totally heterogeneous. It cannot be totally heterogeneous, for that would mean the original event that is recounted would have nothing in common with our present existence. As such it would not be a response in any way to our question. On the other hand, it cannot be totally homogeneous, for it aims at an "absolute beginning" and articulates a "definitive end." It wants to express a certain "before" and a certain "after" that have their own particular status in time and in language. We can see this clearly enough when we try dispassionately to analyze the possibilities of our word. Is it in fact possible to speak by ourselves of the beginning? Can we really dream of saying something true by ourselves about the end, about that future toward which the birth of the world and of the human race is directed? Our language is perfectly adapted to what we are. It is bound to time and space—above all when it has to do with telling a story. But when we speak of origins and the end, we are reaching for something that in part eludes time. Is it possible for us to speak of a beginning before which there was "nothing," an absolute beginning, not relative? And how are we to speak of an end that will not be followed by events homogeneous with those that have gone before? Are we equipped to speak the non-temporal absolute of the beginning and the end?

Can we, for example, speak of the moment when, with the appearance of the human being, nature becomes spirit? To reach that moment, it would be necessary to speak of nature without spirit and before it. But in nature we are penetrated with spirit, and we cannot conceive a "before" because our language itself is manifestation of spirit in nature. In the same way, if we want to express the origin of the universe with a proposition like, "The universe began with a primitive explosion," our language is on the edge of nonsense. In any case it doesn't say what it wants to say. In effect it indicates an origin that comes from something already originated (the primitive atom) and not from an originator; for in this temporal line, by hypothesis, at this point, there is no more originator. The language is trying to reach back to the zero instant, but it cannot "say" it unless this zero instant is actually instant number one. As soon as we reach the furthermost backward point to which we can go, intelligibility vanishes; for what we want to call instant zero is in reality the first of a series, and by definition it should not be circumscribable. We could reason in the same way about the end. We are forced to conclude then that when language tries to recount the beginning, either of nature or of human culture, it cannot reach it because it is itself a part of nature and culture.

All this is true, but what is it saying, finally, if not that we have reached the point in time where the poem is required? Not the time of science, or of fiction, or of rigorous logic, or of pure imagination, but the time of what will be evocation of the birth of the world and of freedom, repeated to God in the festive rendering of thanks and providing the securely moored foundation to every other language. The liturgical poem will thus be *the* radical language, *the* founding word out of which all of history unfolds.

Has the question about origins thus gradually modified itself and become the question of the Word of God? Where does God speak to us of our origins and our end? Where can we hear God speak of these things? Where can we offer to God the acceptance that causes us to be, just as the acceptance of the proper name causes a person to be? And if it is a question of the whole of humanity and of all worlds, who can receive this Word of God for all and render thanks to God in the name of all? It is precisely here, I think, that we must turn to the Eucharist. The Eucharist does not reveal itself as the food and drink of salvation except within an absolutely unique language: a prayer addressed to God in our name by Jesus Christ, who represents us, that celebrates a memorial of the divine covenant and the creation that permit us to be.

The next two chapters will focus on this Word. First we will analyze the development of this unique language, and then we will examine the events it recounts within the prayer it addresses. In a final chapter we will be able to return to the food that is given us in this feast of language.

Notes

1. I would like to underline this point, which shows in its way the primacy of *word* over *language*. There has been considerable reflection on language, its merits and its limits in the last thirty years; but it has perhaps not taken sufficient account of what could be called, in scholastic terms, *the primacy of existence over essence*. This is a twofold primacy: there is no language except an individualized language and, paradoxically, this individuality cannot come to light without the effective act of addressing oneself to another. The structures of language, no matter how they are conceived, sustain this existence even while giving it body. This is why I believe that the words of St. John, "In the beginning was the Word," speak also of the beginning of philosophy. The reflections that follow owe much to the works of Jacques Derrida, *Speech and Phenomena* and Of *Grammatology,* in the sense that I first formulated such reflections many years ago in order to respond to their challenge.

2. Ancient cultures have preserved these differences in their language. See, for example, Pierre Jakez-Hélias, *Le Cheval d'orgueil* (Paris, 1975), 429–33. It is worth noting that in the same

chapter of this book the author speaks of language together with eating and table manners.

3. These reflections, in the end rather simple, reflect the tradition of the major reflections on anguish. One is reminded of Kierkegaard and his concept of anguish as a condition preexisting the fall and determining it. Or there is Heidegger's obsession with the original-original *(originaire)*, by which he meant the origin in so far as it remained present and hidden in development itself. The original-original is never in the already past, for it is always playing secretly in the events of the originated. When a boy looks for his father, he has a presentiment that the paternal score is already a part of what is playing in him. In so far as he cannot believe in a story of his origins, he lacks an essential foundation to balance his language and action. The point I want to underline here is that the resolution of this anguish cannot come from any intellectual effort on the part of the anguished person, but only from the story that is heard and must be believed. St. Thomas said something similar when he said, "If a man wanted to believe only that which he knows, it would be impossible for him to live in this world. *How can someone live if he does not believe anyone? He would not even believe that the man who is really his father is certainly his father*" (*Symbolum Apostolorum*, cap. 1).

4. To borrow the formulations of M. Éliade in *Myths, Dreams, and Mysteries.*

5. Even more there comes into play here the Greek as well as the Christian mystique of the *unknown God.*

6. Books IX and X, passim.

CHAPTER THREE

Eucharist

It could seem exaggerated or off balance to consider the Eucharist as a kind of "Feast of Humanity." Yet, in fact it claims to make present to human living memory that founding event that is the promise of all history, and it does so in such a way that our entire life becomes significant in light of it. The rest of this book, however, will not attempt to prove this point, which in any case, is impossible. Rather, I want to suggest that the Eucharist is at least a response, worthy of faith, to the ultimate question of the meaning of life. The preceding chapters have tried to show that this question affects practices as common as eating and speaking.

Thus the Christian Eucharist would claim to be that primordial and ultimate story that evokes the origin, the development, and the end of every person, of the whole of humanity, and of the whole world. God alone could be the one to whom this story is addressed in an invocation filled with thanksgiving. The Eucharist would also claim to be that festal meal where invocation and evocation become substantial, reaching deep into human flesh. For us to verify these claims in so far as possible, the simplest approach will be to read and comment upon one of the texts of the unprecedented poem that we call the eucharistic prayer. As we do so, we will also keep our attention on the food and drink that are offered and consumed and to which the prayer makes continual reference. The commentary developed here will be done against the background of what I tried to establish in the previous chapters. At the same time, what we discussed in those chapters will find its fulfillment in this eucharistic meditation.[1] I will finish this chapter with a hermeneutical reflection on the level of this eucharistic language.

The General View

INVOCATION

Whoever regards the Eucharist without preconceived notions will immediately be struck by the fact that it appears first of all as an *invocation*. The sense of being a child is recovered in the loving pronunciation of the name "Father," uttered in the very moment when we understand afresh that we are sons and daughters. From among all the possible forms of language and discourse, the Eucharist takes the form of prayer, that is, of thanksgiving and of a communication reestablished. It is not first of all *text,* but rather *voice;* not *statement,* but *address:* "Lord, Holy Father, Almighty and Eternal God." All the other figures of language are inscribed within invocation, which is periodically taken up again and made explicit. The invocative import of the terms employed is more fundamental than the content of what is said. God is the one we invoke in this thanksgiving prayer because God himself first invoked us when he "called" us to be, when he "called" us to freedom in his presence. On the foundation of this invocation we employ other variations in the language—narrative and others—that are not without significance, but all of which take their meaning from within invocation.

As soon as we enter into this perspective of prayer, we are struck again by the importance of the "nonrational" in this address to God. There is an insistence on the use of words that are completely indefinable, such as *holy* or *holiness.* Terms are repeated that indicate attitudes too sweeping to be determined with any precision: *thanksgiving, honor, praise, glory.* The whole text is inscribed within these names, these cries, these acclamations. The beginning is invocation and the end is doxology, that is, "a word of glory." But who can say what *glory* is? The body of the prayer itself is marked throughout with words of the same kind: exclamations that designate, call, exalt, but in the end really want to say "no-thing"; for in fact they want to say "some-one"—God—and to say "everyone"—that is, us. And they say all this in a relationship of ardent reciprocity that is total and, for that very reason, indefinable. They say communion!

Because it is address and prayer, the Eucharist is also song. It is intended that as much of the text as possible be sung, which is not surprising if we remember what we saw above about song as the language of the proper name. Sometimes, if song is absent, the text, no matter how beautiful, risks becoming heavy. For example, in the fourth eucharistic prayer of the Roman Missal, we have a relatively long description of the history of salvation. If recited rather than sung, it loses some of its lyricism. But would we forget that it is God to whom we are speaking? Besides, does God need us to tell him in detail all the good he has done for us? When the priests and the Levites of the Old Testament did this, "they cried out in a loud voice" (Neh 9:4). The eucharistic stories are the epic song of God with human beings. The sacred music of invocation is essential to them.

EVOCATION

In insisting on this invocative aspect of the eucharistic language (address and song), I do not want to reduce its objective referent. The invocation of God is something restored to us. It echoes the Word that has created us and saved us. But within this invocation, in a very sober story where only the essentials have been retained, the Eucharist evokes an event that Christian faith recognizes as the origin and fulfillment of a reconciled humanity toward which all our desire tends. That event is the death and resurrection of Jesus of Nazareth as anticipated in the Last Supper of Christ with his disciples. By remembering before God this real and mysterious story, the Eucharist proclaims that our communion with him passes through this privileged moment. In the same way that we do not enter life until we have accepted our name and the story of our birth as our own, so also we cannot piece together our story as human beings if we do not recognize ourselves before God as born in this event of death and rebirth.

But let us note it well: there is a sort of turnaround here. The human quest in its scientific and mythic forms goes immediately toward the ultimate questions of origins and end. The Christian Eucharist celebrates first an event that is, on the one hand, localized in time, and on the other, marked with the ultimate connotations that we human beings are in need of. The creating act and the final destiny do not appear except in the light of a death and a resurrection. Reciprocally, moreover, the language of origins and of the end belongs to what the founding event says. Here we are most certainly within that total language that must be uttered before being comprehended, and of which our gradual understanding always comes after what our lips have proclaimed.

Evocation is thus essential. Yet our habit of considering the facts in and by themselves is so strong that we tend to think that they are objectively accessible to us apart from the invocative memory that we make of them. This is why I am insisting on this point. We fail to see that we have abstracted the prose of our eucharistic prayer from its lyric and lived context, and we treat it as if it could stand alone. A telling sign of this tendency is the almost exclusive importance until recently accorded, in the eucharistic prayer (not even called "prayer"), to the "institution narrative," which in fact was called rather "the words of consecration." And these words were understood less for their meaning than for their efficacy. This selective insistence has given rise more recently to the inverse temptation: that of reducing the eucharistic words to its elements of communication. We shall return to this point later. Let us now say only this much by way of conclusion: the eucharistic word is situated within an articulation and coordination of invocation and story, and it is precisely this that makes it an existential word. Anything that cripples one or the other of these dimensions is harmful. But so also is anything that subverts the order of the word and wants content to dominate over address.

COMMUNION

Finally, as in every truly human feast, in the Eucharist we exchange food and drink, and the eucharistic word gives these their sense. The desire for total exchange, already inscribed in the invitation to the meal, reaches its fullest realization here, if it is true that food given and offered effectively incarnates in our human flesh today the divine and human covenant that the invocation of our prayer remembers and evokes.

The Third Eucharistic Prayer

A DOUBLE MOVEMENT

First, we will examine a text of the eucharistic prayer, looking at the way in which it refers to God, to human beings, and to things. We will note the registers of language it employs and the content it proposes. Our goal will be to verify in this concrete text the presence and the interplay of the elements of discourse referring to the origin and the end, as discussed in the preceding chapter. In addition, I hope to establish the significance of this discourse when it is addressed to God and accompanied by food and drink. I have chosen the third eucharistic prayer of the Roman liturgy. It is neither the longest nor the shortest of these prayers, but it does perhaps seem to be used a little more often than the others.

If at an earlier stage in the Christian past the eucharistic prayer unfolded in a single movement, the introduction of the *Sanctus* modified its structure. Everything happens now as if there were two introductions into the cycle of the prayer. In a first movement a long *invocation* (Preface), in which different names are given to God, finishes in an acclamation *(Sanctus)*. The *Sanctus* is a shout, an outcry of a community expressing itself in the presence of the God invoked, the God acknowledged as its God. In the interior of the invocation of the Preface, there is a general *evocation* of what God has done for us that culminates in the mystery of Christ.[2] Then we give thanks because this mystery gives us, now and for ever, access to God and allows our *acclamation*. In this way the story becomes a confession of Jesus Christ. This first movement is like the refined essence of the Christian word: invocation, story, acclamation. It is a little like the toast at a banquet where the address to the person being honored includes a selective evocation of his merits and finishes in a salvo of applause.

The second beginning of the prayer has exactly the same structure. After the acclamation of the *Sanctus,* the invocation is begun again and the narration of the story taken up again. This time the story is both more precise and more ample. And the whole finishes in the great doxology that closes the prayer. The difference in the two cycles lies in this: in the first there is a "saying" of the prayer. In the second there is added to the saying a "doing" of the offering and then of the meal. The invocation and the evocation are not confined to the discourse; they apply also to the things that are here and now placed between God and ourselves. The communication between God and human beings, ultimately signified in the mode of invocation, of story, of thanksgiving, passes also and inseparably through bread and wine. The invocation of God is not expressed simply through a brief evocation of Jesus Christ; it is articulated by the food and drink that human beings place here and by the gestures they make—that is, by an *offering*. We will see that it is this term, *offering*, which establishes the link between the language of thanksgiving and the reality of the eucharistic meal. This meal's ultimate potential as meal does not become clear except by means of the invocative and evocative language. Reciprocally, the language of perfect communion with God is not complete apart from a relation, at once practical and symbolic, to certain things. "Earth" is essential to the liturgy.

The more developed aspect of the text and the presence of certain things does not simplify the structure of this second cycle, represented today in the Latin liturgy by the many eucharistic prayers currently in use. It could be said that in this text, no matter how brief, all the registers of human discourse are present and are articulated in rhythms and modalities not easy to analyze. The one constant element is invocation. Everything is addressed to God and said in God's presence. The word never ceases to be addressed, and it continually demonstrates its status as direct discourse, all of whose elements aim at establishing a communication. The eucharistic prayer is thus in the form of communion; and the time that dominates, even if not exclusively, is the present time of communion here and now.

THE STRUCTURE OF THE SECOND CYCLE

In order to uncover the rhythm of this prayer, I would like to draw attention to two phrases that correspond to each other. The prayer begins with a confession of faith that declares the works of God in the present indicative ("You are," etc.), and it says precisely what the expected response is from human beings: *so that from the rising of the sun to its setting a perfect offering may be made to the glory of your name.* This confession of faith in some sense plays the role of exposing the motifs that justify the intercession that immediately follows ("And so, Father,...we ask you..."). This intercession requests a precise action of God on the food and drink brought together here and now on the altar. I will return to the details of these texts as well as to the role of the double narrative and the actions and gestures of Christ that follow the intercession. The point to be made now is that, after this double narrative, we find a prayer of offering that corresponds exactly to what was said at the end of the confession of faith: *we [the people of God] offer you in thanksgiving this holy and living sacrifice.* All that God has done has been done so that God's people could freely make him "a perfect offering." It is this action that "we" are performing now.

We could use the literary term *inclusion* to describe a first major unit of the eucharistic prayer that then starts up again as if it were moving forward on its own strength. It moves with the rhythm of gift offered and given back and of the covenant established through the exchange of food and drink. This is the rhythm, as we saw, that gives to the human meal its ultimate meaning. In this way we know all at once that with God, too, life is a gift: the sacrifice of God and the sacrifice of human beings. And we have some intuition that with God, the "total exchange"—discerned in part but never realized in human gestures of a covenant—can really occur here: divinization and thanksgiving, creation and fulfillment, death and resurrection. This would be the feast of God and of humanity!

Intercession is taken up again, but now its foundation and its object are different. This difference is the principal characteristic of the second major unit of the eucharistic prayer. It is no longer a question of the sanctification of things but of the gathering of peoples. This was the aim from the very start: that the community of human beings might become an offering to God in the covenant that we have remembered. This culmination is requested in words that bring into play first space and then time. It is first a gathering of us here present, who have just made the offering and now ask for unity in our present and for the eschatological consummation of this communion for ever. Then it is a gathering of others, absent from this particular celebration— other Christians, then all human beings, living and dead. The foundation of this request for unity is no longer the general action of the provident creation of God, as it was in the beginning of the prayer. Now the request is made based on the body and blood of Christ that have just been offered.

Finally, in a sort of daring anticipation—as if this complete gathering were already accomplished, uniting the living and the dead, the saints and all the angels—a cry of trinitarian praise closes the prayer because, in the end, the last word cannot be other than a cry of joy and praise. Thus the rhythm of this prayer follows the dimensions of time. It moves from its mysterious roots in the creative action of God all the way through to its realization in the immediate present of a particular celebration. And yet the present celebration is caught up in reference to a past history and in anticipation of an absolute future. The rhythm follows the dimensions of space as well. It moves from the all-embracing "rising of the sun to its setting" to the concrete space of this particular liturgical celebration. In this way it extends the concrete connections of this liturgical space across the whole earth.

Let us take up the text now in its details.

YOU ARE HOLY INDEED...

The opening sentence of the confession of faith forms the transition between the first cycle of the prayer and the second. It takes up again the acknowledgement of the holiness of God that has just been proclaimed in the *Sanctus*, and it bends it toward our world by mentioning creation. Indeed, creation itself expresses its orientation to God in the praise that cries out: *Lord, you are holy indeed, and all creation rightly gives you praise.*

The following phrase develops this confession. We recognize first that *all life, all holiness comes from* God, and that this act of creation and sanctification proceeds from God's interior life and incarnates the eternal processions: *through your Son, Jesus Christ our Lord, by the working of the Holy Spirit.* Even if "things" are sanctified, however, they do not comprise the whole of the activity of God. This activity extends as far as a "people" that is gathered together by God, across time *(from age to age you gather)* and across space *(from the rising of the sun to its setting).* From this gathering God awaits, as a free response to his initiative of creation and salvation, a *perfect offering.* The things created and sanctified by God, Christ, and the Holy Spirit are taken up by the hands of human beings and joyfully given back to their source. God prepares the things and gathers the human beings. If the gesture of offering is the response, then the circle of creation and praise is accomplished in an unending movement. The marvelous exchange *(O admirabile commercium!)* can be achieved between God and the whole creation.

Thus, not only in the interior life of God but also for the creation itself, the law of life is completely and fully operative: the spontaneous bursting forth of being is nourished by what is given away, not by what is kept. We find here what we saw as the deepest meaning of the invitation to the meal and the exchange of words. The same is true between God and human beings: life is covenant—not the covenant of static relations but covenant as a reckless act in which both sides wager all that they are. In giving the gift of life God, so to speak, exhausts the substance of his being for a creation that he brings into being. By a profound necessity, this gift calls for a "perfect offering" in which nothing of creation would be left out of the thanksgiving rendered to the source from which all proceeds. This circle—infinitely and forever!

These themes of creation/sanctification and of the perfect offering give a realistic, incarnated, material resonance to the invocation and praise that form the whole of the first cycle of the eucharistic prayer and whose inspiration remains in the second cycle. Invocation, story, and praise are a work of the lips: they "speak." Offering sacrifice is a work of the hands: the hands "take and lift up" on high what God has created by his hand "bringing down." If creation implies time and space, then its response to God cannot simply be the voice that praises. It must also embrace with the hands the whole of the wide, wide world.

AND SO, FATHER,...WE ASK YOU...

The confession of faith just analyzed here celebrates the action of God on the world of things and of human beings. This is why the words are formulated entirely in the present tense, a present that could be described as "indefinite." The action of God is described without any particular moment or space being precisely designated. All that is said of God here happens now and always, always and now. And so the offering and praise must enter into the majestic domain of this eternal action and reach toward its unfathomable span.

The following prayer effects the passage from the divine action confessed in itself to the liturgical action about to unfold in the "definite" present where we are. We are now going to make to God the "perfect offering." We have just acknowledged the huge compass of God's eternal action, extending across the entire world of things and human beings and across time and space. And so now we ask that this eternal action come into play here and now on the concrete offerings we have brought and on this definite people who we are. We have just acknowledged in a general way that the divine action gives life and sanctifies, and we underlined the mediation of the Son and the Spirit in this. Now we ask that this action become divine consecration and spiritual sanctification of the food and drink placed on the altar. We ask that these be made the body and blood of Christ. The body and blood of Christ will be our *perfect offering*.

Before commenting briefly on the content of this prayer, we should say something about its language. In fact, we have not yet encountered in the text the language of intercession that appears here and that from now on will blend its humble and suppliant tones into the harmony of our prayer. While *invocation* (language's finest pearl) signifies the communion of some sort of equality among the persons who call each other by name, *intercession* (or *epiclesis,* as liturgical vocabulary calls it) develops the difference, the separation, the inequality that the one speaking is incapable of overcoming. Hence the appeal to the kindness of the other to fill the gap. Intercession actualizes those aspects of language that Levinas liked to underline when he spoke of the word as countenance, as coming from on high, as a teaching. In the very moment when the invocation of the name of God aims at perfect communion (signified and realized in the perfect offering), the awareness of our weakness, of our fragility, of some essential deficiency, takes hold of us and causes us to pull back. We put the celebration on hold for a moment so that we might be given the chance to take it up again in another way, more humbly, with a more accurate awareness of God to whom we are addressing ourselves: *And so, Father,...we ask you.* In this perspective, intercession, far from being a partial or marginal element of the prayer, gives it its tone. Certainly it is contained within the praise that began the whole prayer *(All creation rightly gives you praise...)* and the doxology that will conclude it *(Through him, with him, in him...).* And it is inscribed within the celebration of the communion with God. But, by manifesting the inequality of the partners that only the kindness of God addressed by the humility of human beings can overcome, the repetition of the intercessions expresses the climate of grace that pervades the Eucharist. Thanksgiving cannot be rendered *(We give you thanks...)* if something is not first given, and it is not given if it is not expected. The communion between God and human beings, which the whole economy of the eucharistic language manifests, will be transfiguration and divinization. That is why it is asked for at the same time that it is celebrated.

Intercession never ceases to ask that we be able to offer completely, that is, that our acclamation, our giving thanks, our offerings embrace and present what the initial confession of faith designated in a totalizing way: *all creation.* The full invocation of God is not achieved if each and every human being and the whole world are not engaged, and engaged in such a way that their word, thus totalized, attains fully to God and enters into exchange and covenant with him. But how could we who are limited to the small space of the Earth and dispersed along the length of time ever give thanks in a single and full thrust that measures up to the gift that we ceaselessly receive? What are the *gifts we bring* in comparison to the *holy and living sacrifice* required of us? Will not the covenant be impossible in the very moment it is hoped for? Must we repeat the tragic history of sacrifices that fall short of the divinity and so fail to establish the exchange of life? Therefore, for the covenant to be achieved, we must implore it. In the same way that the eternal Word was "abridged" or "contracted" (to borrow the expression of St. Bernard) so that creation might come to be, now conversely creation must be enlarged, must somehow surpass its limits, without ceasing to be itself, so that it can attain the dimensions of the perfect offering. This is why the offerings brought and placed on the altar have to be transformed by the action of the Holy Spirit, just as those who bring them must themselves be transfigured in such a way that in the Spirit there be nothing but an eternal offering. This offering is the body and blood of Christ in themselves, but also in all human beings and in the whole creation. (Here, "body and blood of Christ" refers to his person, to his human individuality, to the mystery of his death and resurrection.) Thus only in this way is there achieved a rendering adequate of word and gesture, of invocation and of what found it. The word expresses the totality and, as this totality is transfigured, the eternal dialogue between God and the divinized creation is inserted into the present of the eucharistic celebration.

The intercession therefore begs for a new intervention of that mediation of Christ and the Spirit that had already been operative in the work of creation. This is why the epiclesis is invoked over very concrete realities: the gifts that we bring. These are not the perfect offering, but by the action of God they can become that. The request is repeated, first in a general way *(make them holy)* and then rendering explicit what we hope for *(that they may become the body and blood of your Son, our Lord Jesus Christ.)*

The Images

The body and blood of your Son, our Lord Jesus Christ.
We should perhaps pause for a moment at these words.
Body and *blood* evoke a violent death, but a violence the
likes of which most people today hardly know through concrete experience. This is not the bloody death that may occur
in war, but rather in capital punishment. It was not so very
long ago that this existed everywhere and that executions
were a public affair. The words of the gospel that speak of
the scourging and the crucifixion of Jesus correspond to
spectacles that the whole world knew in antiquity. In more
recent periods, up to the middle of the nineteenth century, it
was the same for other forms of torture and execution. The
rack, the wheel, the pyre were all part of the urban land-
scape. The relation to a body suffering and blood poured out
pertained to daily culture. This can explain in part the devo-
tion to the passion and wounds of Christ that developed in
the Latin West.[3] There is no need to dwell on this too much.
It would certainly be a mistake, however, to forget the real
referent of these words we say, for they are the images the
eucharistic prayer associates with the name that designates
the very source of life. It is as if the very act of giving life and
sanctifying were identified with the passion of the one who
experiences himself to be violently taken from life. It is as if
in the end giving life and being put to death were a single
gesture.

In one sense, we are not surprised by this. Our analysis
of the invitation to a meal gradually revealed to us that the
very essence of love and covenant consists in giving one's life
so that others may live. Being is achieved in exchange. And
we also saw that the invitation to a meal and the gift of one's
life for others were directed toward the same reality:
covenant. If, then, life is given us, we understand that it is by

means of death. And if we in turn are to give life, death must likewise intervene.

THE INSTITUTION NARRATIVE

The Story: The Fact and Its Meaning

At this point in the prayer we have need of the *story*. The invocation and the intercession call here for a narration that will unveil to us the mystery of the body and blood of Christ, the interplay between his life and his death. We need to understand why and how this body and blood are at one and the same time, in the Holy Spirit, the perfect gift from God and the perfect offering made to God. The communion with God that we seek thus requires the evocation of a precise and particular past, *defined* yet mysterious, where the key to our thanksgiving can be found. In the telling we must make this story come to life again. This is the meaning of the inclusion of story within the eucharistic prayer.

We are not, however, the ones who take the initiative of introducing a story here. At the very point where our word is on the verge of evoking, we find the command of Christ himself who told us to celebrate this mystery. Whence the words: "*Do* this in memory of me." So, not only resaying something but also re*doing*. We have been invited to repeat a symbolic action of Jesus: the meal of the Last Supper. We are invited as well to perceive through this meal what the symbol indicated and what it set in motion; namely, the death and resurrection of Christ as the path toward a perfect covenant with God. The "institution narrative" thus intervenes as the foundation of our plea for the Holy Spirit, expressed in the epiclesis: because Christ has told us to do this and we wish to obey, we beg that the Holy Spirit descend upon our celebration so that we may be able to "do this in memory" and offer the pure and perfect sacrifice, the body and blood of Christ.

As in every story, so here too the telling erases in some sense the temporal distance between what Jesus said and did and what we now recount. A story "re-presents," that is, it takes us back to the past; but even more so, it brings the past to the reality of the present that it may give meaning to our life today. Yet there is more here than the lively presence of a memory gathering a community around an evocation. The word is accompanied by the very gestures of Jesus. We have brought bread and wine to this place, just as the very same were present on the table where Jesus gave thanks. And while we tell again of what Jesus said and did, we ourselves re-do it.[4] The act of pronouncing these words in the present moment of the telling relativizes, so to speak, the aspect of the past in what is recounted. Similarly, the present moment of the gestures, the reality of a doing that expresses and prolongs the saying, creates a new form of presence of the past evoked. Memory is at work here not only through the word and the imagination. Our exterior senses are called into play. The bread of which we speak *is* the bread touched here and now. The wine is what *is* seen here. Not a single word indicates any distance whatsoever between the bread and wine that Jesus used in the past and the bread and wine that we take into our hands now. It is as if time in its temporality were annulled and space denied its dimensions. The reality of the things in our hands is implying that here and now there is happening all that we recount from the past. And, further, if Jesus placed no distance between the bread shared and his body handed over, between the wine offered and his blood poured out, then why would we place any such distance today?[5]

The command of Jesus to repeat his gestures brings more to the fore the dimensions of the present in what we are doing. If in fact every past event, by later being told, can exist in a new dimension of presence in the present, it is certainly not done with a view toward being recounted and evoked by gesture. Of itself it does not set in motion a series of symbolic repetitions. Any event, of course, has the possibility of being later represented; but this does not form part of its inherent structure. By contrast it pertains essentially to every liturgical gesture that is to be repeated. Thus the Last Supper itself is inserted within a tradition of significant meals of the covenant, in the Bible and in the Jewish confraternities of Jesus' time. Yet what is taken up and repeated in Christianity is not simply a holy tradition of mystical meals: it is a particular meal, the last taken by Jesus with his disciples. Everything about it refers to the events that are to unfold on the morrow. This fact confers on the repetition the plenitude of significance and import that were contained in the original. Our Eucharist brings us into the paschal mystery of Christ exactly as the Last Supper did in its precise past. It establishes for us, in our time and space, the eternal covenant, the fruit of this mystery.

The Words and the Liturgical Gestures

Keeping in mind these remarks on the placement and the structure of the narrative within the eucharistic prayer, we can be relatively brief in our examination of the content of the action repeated there. Underlining our gestures with words that are the key to understanding, we repeat a very simple action of Jesus over the bread and wine. In the case of each there are four moments:

- taking (the things)
- giving thanks (to God) and blessing (the things). These are two ways of signifying the same moment of the

action: consecrating the things taken up and referring them to God in thanksgiving.

- giving (to the disciples)
- speaking to the disciples to interpret the gift. First, he says something about what they are to do with it (eat and drink), then, something about the nature of the gift. Here "nature" can be understood as an indication of the reality *(this is)* and an indication of its finality *(handed over for, poured out for).*

This process can be described as having, first, an ascending movement. Jesus takes up the things and directs them toward God. His word addressed to God declares and effects the signification of the food and drink taken in the perspective of the relation of the world to God. This is followed by a descending movement: the food and drink lifted up to God, and thus consecrated, are now given to human beings. The word renders precise just how they are given and with what end in view, for the disciples are invited to take this food in order to seal the bond established with God in the ascending movement and so to enter into the definitive covenant. The term of this double sequence is "the new and everlasting covenant," which is to say that this is a reciprocal and definitive exchange between humanity and God, an exchange by means of which humanity enters into the very movement of eternal trinitarian exchange.

We should observe that this entire process is symbolic. Jesus takes bread, but he speaks of his body. He takes wine but speaks of his blood. There is a dissociation here between the *doing* done in reference to certain things and the *saying* said in reference to others. Yet in reality this dissociation is an affirmation of their unity. Since the word is not content simply to express what is there before our eyes and so indicates something else, it declares that the gestures of lifting up and of gift that are done in reference to the bread and wine in fact are to be identified with other gestures that will be done to the body and blood. For the body will be lifted up on the cross, and from it blood and water will flow. The correspondence is such that whoever enters deeply into what is said and done around the bread and wine will enter just as deeply into what is done to the body and the blood. The one and the other set us on the path toward the perfect covenant. In the end, the one and the other are the same reality. The invitation to the meal *is* the opening of Christ's side, which seals his death and opens life. The bread broken *is* the body handed over. The wine *is* the blood poured out. What Jesus says at the supper is thus totally unique because in his discourse concerning the bread and the wine and in his actions with them, he aims at and actually attains another and yet identical dimension of the mystery, that of his body and blood offered.

Anamnesis

If we take now in a single glance the entire movement of the prayer from the initial confession of faith, we see that it unfolds in the atmosphere of an intense presence. We begin in the "indefinite present" of the action of God, which called in turn for a continual and perfect offering on our part. Then the plea for the power of the Holy Spirit has as its object the realization in our "definite present" of the *holy and living sacrifice* offered in thanksgiving to God the creator and savior. This power is exercised through the narration that follows the plea and that recalls a "definite past" that transfigures our present. This transfiguration derives from the very nature of story: from the repetition of the gestures recounted, by its reference to the command that enjoins *this* repetition, from the meaning and reality of the words pronounced by Jesus and the gestures accomplished. We find ourselves here within an arrangement of time without equal. The *past* of the mystery of Christ so profoundly invades the *present* of our celebration that it is the same mystery that we can *now* offer to God. This establishes the realm of covenant that permits us the perfect invocation of the name. Under the form of holy foods given as sign and reality of the covenant, the eucharistic story evoked bread as a body handed over and wine as blood poured out. Now in the prayer called the "anamnesis," immediately following the institution narrative, we translate this into personal terms *(we call to mind the death your Son endured for our salvation)* and into mysterious events that elicit in us a waiting *(the death your Son endured for our salvation, his glorious resurrection and ascension into heaven, and ready to greet him when he comes again)*. This translation or interpretation of the story and its gestures establishes the possibility of a gesture on our part where we now offer the realities commemorated, found symbolized and represented in the gifts on the altar *(we offer you in thanksgiving this holy and living sacrifice)*.

The cycle of the prayer is not totally completed, however. From the memory of Christ and the offering of his mystery, we must now pass to the effect of this memory in us.[6] To remember means to make our own what is remembered and to invest in it. After all, Christ did all this only for our sake so that we might be incorporated into his personal gestures. It is for this reason that as soon as the intercession concerning the pure sacrifice is complete (whose axis is entirely christological), a second great epiclesis is immediately begun. This epiclesis is situated explicitly *between* the pure sacrifice of Christ's body and blood and the sacramental communion in the food and drink laid out on this altar. What it requests relies on Christ's act and the offering of it that we can make through the holy gifts *(Look with favor on your Church's offering)*. It anticipates the consent of the disciples who celebrate this Eucharist today by eating his body and drinking his blood in the transfiguration of the Spirit. *(Grant that we, who are nourished by his body and blood, may be filled with his Holy Spirit, and become one body, one spirit in Christ.)* The prayer declares the meaning of the approaching sacramental communion, and it asks for its completion in us. We pray that we may be able to respond to the gift Christ has given us by the gift of our very selves. We pray that the living and holy offering of the body and blood of Christ will be extended to the spiritual offering of the community that celebrates, united in love by the Spirit. It is a double request joined to the anticipated eucharistic communion: a request that we become one body and one spirit, a request that we ourselves become the spiritual offering. This double request is made in the perspective of the final consummation already evoked in the anamnesis and taken up again in the prayer that puts us in communion with all the saints in heaven *(an everlasting gift to you)*.

The memorial and the offering do not yet stop here. If the body and blood of Christ are the perfect offering that gathers together space and time, then the memorial must extend to those who are not present at what we are doing here and now, for they too are implicated in this reality. Thus the communion will be total when we invoke God. This is why we make a memorial of the living and the dead at this point in the prayer. Then all these can be taken up into the final doxology of the prayer, which embraces every offering in thanksgiving and in the acclamation that gives glory to God. The offering has become again word and cry, but a word that now includes the bodily totality of Christ, that is, the whole of humanity and the whole world.

Then the action of eating this body (which is handed over to us and which we offer to God) and of drinking this blood (which is poured out for us but which we receive for God) seals even in our bodies the eternal covenant.

The Christian Feast

A question arises at this point. As can often happen in trying to explore and develop the meaning of a doctrine and a practice, we suddenly notice, with a certain fear perhaps, that we have gone far beyond where we started our thinking. A perfect invocation of God, a perfect offering, perfect praise, mystery of body and blood, of bread and wine, story, acclamation—are we really in the truth with this kind of thought? Or have we not perhaps strayed, certainly without wanting to, into some sort of imaginary, poorly demythologized world?

Eucharist: Fulfillment of the Potentials of Exchange and Word

What we developed in the preceding chapters and the conclusions reached there can quiet our doubts concerning this way of speaking about the Eucharist. There we spoke about fundamental, elementary human behaviors, about food and the word. At the end of the chapter on the word, we saw that all human languages are necessarily inscribed within a word that has no common measure with all others: the word concerning origins and the end. We insisted that such a founding word cannot be uttered except within the context of the feast and that it has its own proper characteristics. The language of origins and the end cannot be a scientific language, in which "science" means relentless, logical rigor. It cannot be mythic, for it does not separate the beginning and the end from developments within these poles, as myth does. It is not projected into a fantasy time prior to the appearance of evil and death, as myth is. Scientific language, too homogeneous with our everyday existence, cannot speak of the beginning and the end but only of a certain number of structures limited by time and space. Mythic language, too separated from our everyday existence, provokes static and regressive behaviors that want to exorcise not only evil but also time. In reality, the true language of origins and the end is a story of a unique type, both a narrative and a poem, suggesting the original moment when all things burst forth and the end where all will be reconciled and accomplished. It pertains to the truth of this language that it be addressed in invocation of the one from whom all things come and toward whom all things are going. The paradox is that, thanks to this "story–prayer," however different it may be from all the other language we produce, our word and our action have been set free for the time and space in which we find ourselves, a time and space in which we are meant to speak and to act. In fact, we receive time and space from the one who gives them to us in the Eucharist, and we begin to move within them in communion with him and with one another.

No festal word is uttered, however, if human beings do not celebrate with their bodies and their senses, if they do not signify, by mutual exchange of what they have produced for life, the communion that comes not only from sharing but from a reciprocal process of losing what one has in order to receive what is offered. Our analysis of food seen on its different levels of daily life brought us to this understanding. The festive exchange of foods is the support for the solemn exchange of words. The truth of this is measured by the extent to which we venture what we have and risk ourselves in hope.

Now, the Christian Eucharist exactly displays the characteristics of a festal word addressed. It is addressed to God and joined to a liturgy of offering that is at the level of what is said. Within a framework where invocation never ceases, it evokes the original and ultimate event, the paschal mystery of Christ. It envelopes this invocation and evocation within an offering where all, finally, is exchanged between God and human beings: the body and blood of Christ as the totality of the world and of history. By that very fact, the Christian Eucharist frees human beings to make history. It unchains them from any immobilizing mythology, and it allows them to deploy their intelligence and their freedom in a space and time that are no longer without meaning but that instead are open to their own transfiguration.

Eucharist: The Beginning and the Middle of Time

The Christian Eucharist displays an original element in comparison with what a merely human word might be or what a feast of origins and end might offer. The story the Eucharist tells and celebrates is not situated in those chronologically unreachable times of the absolute beginning and the ultimate end. It does not directly evoke the beginning and end of the world and of time. Instead, it tells of events which in part at least we can comprehend and even date to a particular given moment within the whole of history, namely, the life, death, and resurrection of Jesus of Nazareth. But can these events really pertain to the mystery of origins and of the end? Can the creation and the fulfillment of the world really be remade in Jesus of Nazareth? With these two questions we have arrived at the point where Christian faith shows itself precisely as *faith* and where no demonstration is possible. We can only offer our "yes" as response to these questions. Nothing can prove that Jesus of Nazareth, dead and risen, is the "alpha and omega." Yet if the confession of faith that Jesus is Lord takes up those human behaviors most closely tied to the whole of our desire, our language, and our body and if it sets them free, then it is certainly not unreasonable to risk joining those multitudes who have made him the center of their lives. The truth of this confession of faith and its risk will be verified by the freedom that it gives to enter into the total exchange between God and humanity.

Putting faith in Jesus is not the celebration of a closed past that perpetuates itself only in the remembering of it. The story that this faith contains has in view a unique event whose description cannot be compared with any other event, past, present, or future. In fact, it treats of death and resurrection, which is to say, a beginning and an end. Considering this mystery in its unity—death *and* resurrection—Christian tradition speaks of it as "the fullness of time" or time's "fulfillment." (This is eschatological language, for it is language of an end.) Simultaneously, it speaks of it as a "new creation." (This is language of origins, for it speaks of a beginning.) Our story therefore is situated within this limit zone of language that I spoke about in the previous chapter. The way in which we use words to describe an event completely contained within time will not work here. In reality, we cannot actually speak of death in this way because we have not yet died. Still less can we speak of resurrection, because that is the realization of a new world. Yet the relative impotence of our language does not constitute a sufficient reason to cast into doubt the reality of what we evoke. Rather, it is the contrary. The death and resurrection of Jesus are of a reality so dense that we cannot "say" them perfectly with our words; we can only evoke and suggest them. We cannot reduce them to the measure of our rationality—that would be science. We cannot have them wander away to a region totally estranged from what we are, human beings of flesh and blood. That would be myth. We are speaking of an actual death and an actual resurrection. These become "historical" in our language in the same way that the beginning and the end that give meaning to the temporal unfolding of reality can be "historical." In part, beginning and end lie beyond this unfolding; in part they pertain to it. So also with Jesus' death and resurrection. Finally, this unique location of the paschal event, in its reality and in our language, allows us to believe that the evocation of it in the Eucharist renders it present in a way that is also unique: not only as a memory but as reality still.

In the same way, the exchange of food joined to the festive confession of faith in Jesus should not be reduced to just any sort of exchange. In fact, very little is present; we have just a little bread and a little wine. But this little contains all, for with it we profess the presence of the perfect offering, the body and blood of Christ. What no exchange of food or gifts could realize *is* realized in the Christian Eucharist: total loss of self for the giving of life and absolute hope for receiving it. In the Eucharist, the materiality of the gift is at the level of the event confessed.

We will understand better the proper status of the eucharistic word and food if we spend some time now reflecting on the event remembered in the liturgy: the death and resurrection of Jesus of Nazareth. We will seek to respond to several questions. How can such an event be considered as founding in the same way that origin and end are founding? Is there some way of achieving here a certain verification of our faith, of procuring some understanding of this mystery, which in its turn would bring us to a renewed celebration of and a more thoughtful entry into the covenant and into history opened up by it?

Notes

1. From the moment when it is a question of dealing with a *text,* whether it be a literary, biblical, or liturgical text, the question of method is posed. My reading will be primarily a literary one. On the one hand, this will involve an analysis of structures and the correspondences in the text, as well as a tracing of its movement. On the other hand, it will involve attention directed to the symbols that come into play. This choice is suited to the challenge posed in this book. It supposes, however, a certain knowledge of the history of texts, though here it is employed as a sort of safeguard against flights of fantasy in the interpretations. Historical-critical studies of the anaphoras, now as in the past, follow a different method, though it could be said that they arrive at substantially the same conclusions, even while the nuances and harmonies that come to the fore will be different. When there is a "text," there are "infinite interpretations." The choice of one method is not a condemnation of others but simply the claim that it is possible with this method to arrive at insights not otherwise possible. The hermeneutic is both single and plural.

2. This general evocation, which constitutes the core of the Preface, can include a particular insistence on one or the other aspect of the mystery of Christ according to the feast celebrated, or a reference to the Blessed Virgin or the saints, but always recapitulated in the light of the mystery of Christ.

3. I would add that the images of violence that are so widely diffused by television do not have the same impact. They are retransmissions and virtual, and as such create a different type of distance in relation to the effectively real. It could be noted that, paradoxically, if young people had more *real* images of death (violent but also natural and normal death), they would be less prone to violence.

4. In fact there is such incertitude about the nature and exact unfolding of the Last Supper of Jesus with his disciples that we cannot pretend literally to be reproducing the exact gestures of Jesus as he would have done them. Such a literal reproduction would not, in any case, necessarily be meaningful. What we do is

thoroughly *symbolic* of what Jesus did, in the same way that the narratives of the Eucharist in the New Testament return us to the meal of Jesus through an interpretation of its meaning.

5. There is in the telling of every story—and to a maximum degree in the eucharistic telling—a delicate figure of duration that continues to run while we are celebrating and yet is also somehow annulled. It is this figure that is expressed in the biblical word meaning *memorial*. Yet more generally, this seems an essential part of any authentic philosophy of time.

6. I present here a commentary on the second part of the second cycle of the prayer. This commentary will be brief because the text does not involve the complex anthropological and theological questions that come into play in the christological part of the prayer.

CHAPTER FOUR

Death and Resurrection

I want to begin this chapter by insisting from the outset that no historical or theoretical reflection on the death and resurrection of Jesus Christ can attain to the fullness of reality and significance that these events take on when they are remembered in the eucharistic liturgy. I have already said why: the truth of a story is not independent of the person to whom it is addressed or of the situation of the one telling it. In the eucharistic prayer we address ourselves immediately to God by telling a story as old as Christianity itself, a story repeated through all the Christian generations on the foundation of the apostolic witness. In the Spirit, who inspires us, this story renews the event that we consider a founding event. Further, this eucharistic prayer is not merely a work of the voice. It concretely employs real foods and a festal meal through which the gift of God and the response of faith simultaneously become flesh. In this context of presence and of life, the death and resurrection of Jesus are not objects of investigation but rather a proclamation that liberates our history and opens before us today the freedom bequeathed by the truth of time. Thus, the place where the paschal mystery is recounted with the greatest truth and the most realism is not in a theology book or in catechetical instruction. These come before or after, but they only have value when joined to the living invocation of God, which is never as full as it is in the Eucharist. The true history is a poem of thanksgiving.

In the same way, the eucharistic celebration assumes a real primacy over scripture itself, even if scripture enters in a number of ways into the celebration. Scripture, even if inspired, always yields to the word and the rite, which are likewise inspired. Thus, the gospel stories yield to the liturgical story, and we do not have to subordinate the all-embracing truth and weight of reality in our eucharistic celebration to a critical examination of the apostolic testimonies of the death and resurrection of Jesus. Rather, it is the opposite that is true: never is the story a more true proclamation than in its memory celebrated in the Eucharist.

The Church has always celebrated the "breaking of the bread." In the story of the disciples on the road to Emmaus, St. Luke specifies that it is here that the Lord makes himself known. When the breaking of the bread takes place, the explanation of the scriptures that Jesus had made along the road becomes clear, but not before.[1] Besides, the gospels themselves are not "historical archives." They are written syntheses inspired by faith in the resurrection of Jesus, destined to sustain and clarify the life of this or that community. If often enough, just in virtue of the very beauty of their content, the gospels awaken in a reader, even an indifferent one, a response of profound sympathy, and if they sometimes set in motion a true process of conversion, still the figure of Jesus does not appear in all its plenitude except to those who celebrate today in the liturgy the faith of those who wrote the gospels and of those for whom they were first written.

The gospels may not be historical archives, but neither are they mythological stories. Even if they reconstruct events in such a way as to make a particular meaning clearly emerge, neither the letter of the text nor the faith with which we surround it permits us systematically to cut off from it whatever would pertain to a story considered as homogeneous to other histories of great men. Such a homogeneous story, however, which indicates its human and temporal dimensions, is located within a more all-embracing sequence, that of universal history. In its turn, in order to speak of the beginning and the end, this sequence requires the use of a language that, while wanting to avoid being mythic, is nonetheless located at the limit of the possibilities of any language. In certain of its traits the language of the gospels finds itself, in fact, at this limit, as when it speaks of death and resurrection. Yet, in other aspects, the gospel language simply evokes everyday human situations. That is the unique mystery of these four writings, the mystery that we totally assume in the eucharistic celebration. There is, therefore, a constant coming and going between the "sacred mysteries" and the "sacred scriptures."

Another remark is required here at the beginning of our brief investigation of the death and resurrection of Jesus. If the resurrection had not been attested to by the disciples of Jesus, we would scarcely be interested in his life and death. We would only be interested somewhat in his teachings, and it is difficult to say to what extent. The life and death of a teacher of wisdom only have a relative importance compared to the doctrine and use of it that we can make today. But if Jesus is proclaimed as risen from the dead, then something truly new and completely unheard of is produced in him. Thus our attention is drawn back to his person. His life and death appear as tightly linked to his message and to his true personality as well. The centuries-long meditation of the Church on Jesus Christ is thus entirely joined to the resurrection as its point of departure.[2] The diversity of traits with which this meditation can be clothed is correlative to the interpretation given to the announcement of the resurrection. So, I consider here the death and the resurrection of Jesus as two faces of the same event, which complete and clarify one another.

The Death of One Person and the Death of Others

Recognizing that the importance of the death of Jesus is revealed to us by the reality of his resurrection does not, however, lead to the conclusion that this death was so unique that a general reflection on the nature of death would yield no results. On the contrary: If the death of Jesus was the death of a man, then, what we know about death in general should help us to understand this particular death. Nowadays death is the object of numerous reflections. Psychoanalysis has clarified its symbolic value for the individual. Sociology and the history of customs and religions have clarified its symbolic value in human communities. Reflections on the concrete experience of death, in the hospital or elsewhere, as well as on euthanasia, have for their part led to what might be called a modern renewal of the *ars moriendi*. I would like to take some direction from this contemporary cultural work in order to offer an initial clarification of the human reality of the death of Jesus.

In the perspective of the human sciences, death can only be viewed from the perspective of the living who remain. What is observed is what the death of someone provokes in the survivors and what can be concluded from this about the human reality, and more precisely perhaps, about the human body. In fact, this perfectly fits our problematic, for what we know about the death and resurrection of Jesus comes to us entirely from the testimony of the apostles, that is, from their personal and communal experience of Jesus dead and risen. Thus, what I want to recall briefly here is ordered to a deeper reception of the apostolic testimony.

THE LIVING AND THE DEAD

In reality we know nothing of death. It is non-knowing par excellence. It fills with holes our otherwise flawless intellectual and affective constructs, unless, of course, our awareness of death helps us at least to avoid the temptation of arranging everything as if death did not exist. If we try that, then death becomes the blind point that silently polarizes our precarious efforts to live.

What we do know is that the death of someone else is in part our own. We are taking note of a rupture when we say, "he breathed his last," or "he is dead," or "it's all over." But this rupture affects us as well. Certainly it does so differently from the way it affects the one who has died, yet perhaps in its own way just as much. Let us look more closely at those moments that immediately precede and follow the death of another. We are there while an oppressive agony extends and makes us—who are ourselves in agony—ask, when will it end? The sound of that breathing coming at an ever more difficult pace marks our experience of the other's death. Up until that moment we existed together, and through his living body a whole series of relationships developed and intertwined with us. Now he is there still, but it is as if he were no longer there. His body is no more than a spent machine, and we are waiting for it to stop. Every one of its pulsations destroys something in us as well, that which in us lived from him and for him. His body little by little is becoming a corpse, and this destruction attacks head-on what was most personal in our lives together. *Physical* death is a *human* rupture. We understand this well perhaps from the example of euthanasia, which may be as much a remedy for the anguish of the living as a relief of the suffering of the dying. We do not want the other to suffer, but part of the reason for that is because another's suffering is unbearable for us. When the moment comes when we must say, "It's all over," we know well that something will be finished in us also. From that moment forward nothing more will ever be exchanged with the one who has died. Certain tones in my voice will never be heard again. Certain gestures with my living body, I will make no more. Certain expectations of my mind and heart will never be fulfilled again. In the final analysis, even before being an event in the history of another, isn't death in one sense first of all the wound inscribed in us by the disappearance of someone who counted in our sight? It is because something has died in us that we can intuit a little of what death was for the one we loved. Sometimes, a sickness can follow our mourning. This is experiencing in ourselves something of the biological destruction that underlies the rupture of human relationships.

The Funeral Rite

Let us not leave the deathbed too quickly. The breathing has stopped, and, look, little by little the tormented features of the face so recently in agony begin to repose. It is as if the dead one were sleeping. Although we know perfectly well that it is impossible, we half wait for the closed eyes of this tranquil face to open again. We find asleep the body and the features of the one who just shortly before was awake and was the center of life for all who gathered round. Yet— incomprehensible to us!—the eyes will never open again and there will be no response to what our living bodies would want to continue to convey to the dead body. This waiting for a life that is not coming back is a sign to us of just how much this life was a part of ours.

The funeral itself will underline these feelings. We are going to consign to the earth the one we have lost, for we know well that this corpse will decompose, and we could not watch this. The biological cycle in which the dead one participated while alive and over which in part some control was exercised, now takes charge of the one who is dead. There is nothing to do but deliver what remains to the earth. Nonetheless, to this body become corpse and given over to the rhythms of nature, we offer a funeral bath. Up until the last moment we honor it. It is perhaps not logical, but it is profoundly true. We are not denying that from now on everything will move in the direction of dissolution, and we recognize here and now the organic reality of every human body; namely, sooner or later, its mortality. Yet the body still carries the features of the one who was a living body, the features of a someone. So we do for her what she can no longer do for herself, but which she did so often with us: she dressed herself and presented herself. This is our last expression of the desire that the presence of the one already gone awakens in us! It is also an intuition—much stronger in ancient cultures than in our secular ones—that in death not all is dead, that to treat the dead in some way like the living is to recognize another dimension of death: that is, perhaps death is not only what it seems to be and life in reality is "not taken away but transformed," as a text from the Latin ritual suggests.

Bravely Bearing Grief

So, the death of another is indeed in part also our own death. This does not mean that this experience will necessarily be marked by an anguish that never abates. The wounds scar over, more or less; and the memory of the loved one gradually becomes a discreet presence in a life that will be reorganized without the one who has died. Do we not in fact experience a certain unease with people who do not really seem to have accepted a death and who do not accept that something has also died in them? They try to live with their dead as if they were still alive, and this distances them from their present. The same unease is associated with an overly strong interest in mysterious communications that supposedly arrive from the beyond. Death is a wound in us. We must consent to it. In that way we live again and survive. We intensify existing relationships; we create new ones; we find a balance again in our body and in our language. We cannot bring our dead back to life. The true faithfulness consists in continuing to live ourselves, but without them, or at least without the bodily and speaking presence of the one who had been indispensable to us.

DEATH: REVEALER OF THE BODY

We can draw these reflections together by trying to put into relief what they suggest to us about the human body—the body of the dead, the body of the still living. When we spoke earlier about food, we already perceived the paradox of the body and the difficulty of expressing it with exactitude. Two things must be maintained at the same time. First, that the embodied human being participates in a rhythm not under an individual's control, a rhythm where earth, air, fire, and water are all engaged. And yet, though always in a body, the human being is also distanced from these elements. The *human* way of being corporeal is to be both completely plunged into this biological substratum and also distant from it. The upright stance is the sign of this unique situation. The human being is held up by the earth and cannot be freed from it, and yet nothing comes to the body except through the hand, guided by language. The body of a man or woman is never just a thing, even if there are certainly "things" in them. The life of a human being unfolds from the balance between the elements of the body and that which is more than element.

If we turn to the level of human encounters, it is also clear here that a living body is never perceived only as a body, as an element. It is never perceived apart from the signs it produces, the contacts it realizes, its continual exchanges not only with the earth but also with other living bodies. These are persons who encounter one another. Nonetheless, no relation is ever realized except within a biological substratum with which we are in continual dialogue for life and for health. The two aspects are, in fact, but one. Physical illnesses are often the corporeal expression of anguish in human encounters, just as the lack of human encounter can result in unhealthy organic functioning.

Death occurs at the moment when the body ceases to be a body with and for others, but at that same instant it ceases to be a human body on the earth. It is no longer the living unity in the rhythm of a living nature. It is no longer a body but a corpse that must be placed in the earth. As for those who surround the deathbed, they are still bodies. Their size, their weight, their real or apparent health all witness to it. They surround this one who "is no more." But they are bodies also by means of all that their relations with the one now dead had inscribed in their bodies. Something of their own bodies is therefore also dying here. And who could raise it up again?

These brief reflections on "the death of someone, the death of others" underline that a person does not die alone. Into her death she draws something of the life of others, at least of those who have really been joined to her. It is even by means of whatever dies in us that we can perceive something of the mystery of the death of the one who has totally passed beyond us. Would it also be possible to come to the conclusion that if someone were to rise again, he would not rise alone? Already we experience that if people close to us manage to escape from a long, painful illness and the day comes that they are clearly out of danger, we ourselves feel that we are somehow returned to life. So, what would it be if we are talking now of Jesus Christ?

The Death and Resurrection of the Community

Before looking at what the death of Jesus itself may have been, if that is possible, we can recognize, following the logic of these reflections, what it was for the community that experienced it. This community existed entirely thanks to the person of Jesus. Its members were the disciples of the master, children of the prophet, the young enthusiastic force (already tried and persevering, John 6:67–69) of the one who was going to restore the kingdom of God. Jesus had gathered these men by the strength of his language, his attitudes, his way of being, his deeds of power and his humility. In short, he gathered them by a radiance and an operation of which his body had been the principle. The effect of his arrest, of the "seizing of his body," had naturally been the reverse: their dispersion. When he dies and is taken down from the cross, Jesus' corpse is like the sign of the state of the community: a motionless and silent body, cut off from human relation with the world and with others, fit only to be rendered to the earth. Among the disciples—can we still speak of a community?—a mortal sadness reigns, of which certain scenes in the gospels preserve the echoes: sadness at having lost, shame for not having followed. With all this, very prosaically, very humanly, the followers of Jesus feared for their own lives. Already before the death of Jesus, they had fled; and Peter had denied him. Afterward, there are the locked doors of the hiding place where these men had fearfully gathered, now deprived of their reason for existing together. Just as the lifeless body of Jesus is sealed in the tomb, so also the community, bereft of any interior breath, is closed in a room, waiting for those who constitute it to slip away furtively, one by one, without being noticed. What could have kept them joined to one another, since the one who had gathered them was dead, and his death had made die in them their being his disciples and the mission they had received from him? Each one would return to his own home, carrying in his heart a wound—that of an immense hope incomprehensibly deceived, of a bitter memory of the man they loved and of companions who for some months had believed in him. Thus, the death of Jesus coincided with the death of his group because it was the relation of the disciples to him and among themselves that vanished in the moment when he breathed his last.

Oddly, however, the community continued. It did not just hold together for a certain time, like one or other of the Old Testament "schools of the prophets," preserving for several decades the memory of a man of God and especially the text of his words, the content of his teaching and its inspiration. The community of Jesus kept its awareness of its mission for the kingdom. It developed to the point of making a continual "memorial" of him and of believing that it had the promises of life eternal and thus a universal mission in space as well as in time. And despite the problems and divisions present from the start, this community survived the ravages of time. It is still alive among us. Just when the death of Jesus, involving the brutal interruption of his work and the final failure of his mission, should have had the result also of the death of his group, that group showed itself to be quite alive. Does not this "resurrection" of the community bring us then to the "resurrection" of Jesus himself? Is not this transfiguration of the community, in its extension and in its ideal, the prolongation of the transfiguration of Christ?

APPEARANCE AND DISAPPEARANCE

So, there is an exact parallel between the fate of Jesus and that of his community. I would like to explore this theme more deeply by studying the idea and the reality of "appearance." There is much discussion about the reality or otherwise of the appearances of the risen Jesus to his disciples, as if the meaning of the word itself were completely clear.[3]

It is necessary to return to the phenomenon of the glance, the look, and to the phenomenon of seeing it. That which appears can be looked at and seen. In chapter 2, in our discussion about the word, I recalled that Levinas compared the word to a countenance: not a mere bodily face that can be stared at as one stares at a thing, but a countenance whose position "from above" is respected, which gives itself to be seen, and which is not meant to be stared at. In reality in our first looking at another we are always tempted to stare, guided more or less by intensity of interest or curiosity. This first looking carries with it a question to the effect of, "How is she made, who is she like?" which is very close to an even more neutral question: "How is it made, what is it like?" This way of looking has something destructive about it: it undresses, it takes to pieces, it stares. If we are not careful, when we have stared too hard, no countenance will remain, neither the countenance of the other whom our look has reduced to a thing, nor a countenance turned toward us, for we will have destroyed the hidden mystery that the face exposed, even though it had not unveiled its full mystery.

We stop staring in that moment when a hidden beauty forces us to stop and when its very radiance breaks our egoism. And perhaps this happens most often when our indiscreet and curious looking meets the glance of the countenance stared at: its surprise, its being disarmed, its indignation, but, in the best instance, its glance cast kindly toward us, not staring at us. Such a glance pierces our façade just when our insistence remained powerless to pierce the other. Such a piercing is full of gentleness, to the point of transforming our own look and provoking the appearance of our true countenance. When Nathaniel was invited to "come see" Jesus, he probably came with the look of the curious, but it was enough for Jesus to look at him for the encounter to be different (John 1:45–51). Here we have the reverse of Levinas' comparison. He had said that the word is like a countenance. But the countenance that looks and is looked at is also like a word. It is complete expression, both a creative address and a passivity that waits to be created by the glance of the other.

The Countenance of Jesus

As long as they were with Jesus, the disciples were living and learning this modification of looking, this transfiguration of the face. However, two things probably kept them from reaching the depth of this manifestation. On the one hand, their deepest desire seems to have been concentrated on the restoration of Israel and its glory as the chosen people, freed at last from its humiliation. Thus a preconception surrounded the manifestations of Jesus and their own understanding of themselves. Their fixed ideas about the salvation of Israel functioned as a filter or an interpretive grill for all that they saw and heard. As St. Paul says, a veil covered their heart, which prevented the total penetration of their glance (2 Cor 3:14–16). They wanted so much for the Messiah to have a certain aspect that they could not fully see the reality of Jesus. The second obstacle was the simple fact that Jesus was always visible and tangible in their midst. Nothing ever stopped them from fixing their eyes on him and drawing him to themselves. Simply by his presence Jesus was available to their desires and to all the questioning that these might elicit. He was always there. And so because of this constant availability and because of the preconceptions that subtly oriented their glance, the disciples never went as far as the ultimate reality that the countenance of Jesus was manifesting.

The death of Jesus snatched the master from the glance of his disciples. His body had been taken down from the cross and sealed in the tomb. With this, the messianic hopes of the community were also destroyed, and the meeting of the disciples would be as short-lived as the body of Jesus, which was now given over to corruption in the hollow of the rock. The two obstacles that had prevented the disciples from turning a proper intensity of their glance toward Jesus—their preconceived ideas about the kingdom and the always available bodily presence of Jesus—were now removed. Yet Jesus is no longer there, and his community is on the verge of definitive dispersion. The disappearance of the obstacles can do no good!

THE APPEARANCES AND THE COMMUNITY

It is precisely here, I think, that the mysterious phenomenon of the appearances of Jesus after the resurrection awakens in us, in a very refined and delicate way, faith in the resurrection. What is essential in the appearances is that Jesus *lets himself* be seen again. I want to highlight this expression: *lets himself*. A living man doesn't let himself be seen: he *is* seen because he is visible. If it happens that he hides himself, it is precisely because he is visible and wants in some particular circumstance to cover over this visibility.

Unable to suppress it, he simulates it. But the risen Jesus has gone beyond this alternative of visible/invisible. When he appears, *he* summons and commands his own visibility. When he invites his disciples to touch him, *he* renders himself tangible for them. But he also disappears just as he appears. He *lets himself* be seen by some and not by others. Everything happens as if from now on the person of Jesus had penetrated his own body with such mastery that he can now render it visible or not to others, tangible or not to others. The looking of Jesus is now a looking that constitutes itself as looking. His body constitutes itself as body, in itself and for his disciples. In its turn, this unheard-of novelty prolongs and modifies among the disciples all their looking, hearing, and interpretation of Christ. The disciples turn their glance on Jesus and hear his voice, not at any moment they want, as they did before his death, but only in so far as Jesus *lets himself* be seen and heard. The relation of the disciples with the countenance and the body of Jesus is certainly very real. They look, they touch, they hear. But this is entirely subordinated to "the wish of the Other." Jesus is now truly the other, because he alone among all human beings controls even the manifestation of his own body to others. He is not an other that one can find by looking for him. He is not found unless his desire causes him to *let himself* be seen. Then, apart from anyone's searching, he manifests himself in his body, a manifestation totally dependent upon the pure desire to communicate. No one has power over this desire but Christ himself.

The Resurrection of the Community

The appearances continue and, all at once, they change the relation of the disciples to Christ. These appearances are going to reestablish the community that was on the point of falling apart. But it will be different from the past, for the manner of Christ's presence has changed and, as a consequence, the look of the disciples has changed. More precisely, they have been given an entirely new looking and an entirely new hearing in the spirit of the risen Lord. While discovering the absolute mastery of Jesus, they also experience themselves as ever more capable of a new glance toward him and their very bodies occupied by a new relationship to him. Previously, life together had created apparently solid bonds between Jesus and his disciples, based as they were on the undeniable consistency of tangible contact, even if this contact was fragile because it was always threatened by death. Now the appearances establish a new regime. They testify to the power of Jesus over his body and his control of its manifestation. They demolish the fragility that belongs to the perspective of death. Conversely, they also eliminate the ease of immediate tangible contact in favor of a new depth that reaches into the very bodies of the disciples, the depth of looking and of hearing created by the light and voice of Christ who appears to them. The new community is no less real, no less tangible than it was formerly. They are the same men gathered around the same Christ, but what unites them to him and to one another is no longer the same. The appearances give the measure of this transfiguration and this new creation.

There is also the word of the risen one. Jesus, in the midst of his disciples, did not stop teaching and sending. The risen Lord not only appears; he also speaks. He confirms the truth of his appearances by affirming his identity, which will open the way to continual reflection on his person and mission. But most importantly, Jesus breathes his Spirit onto his disciples so that they can grasp what they are the witnesses of. He gives his Spirit so that, having become apostles of the risen one by their experience of seeing him and hearing the authority of his word, they might proclaim what they have seen and heard. The paschal experience transfigures their vision, but it also unfolds into testimony: the new creation that the apostles have seen and that they begin to recognize in themselves becomes, by the word of Christ and through the gift of his Spirit, responsibility for the world, even if the apostles needed time to take the full measure of the reality they had received in the paschal mystery.

The Disappearance

The appearances remake the community gathered around Christ and reveal its transfigured reality. This happens positively because the disciples receive a new capacity to look on Jesus and to hear his definitive words. But the community is also gradually being remade negatively in that the appearances eventually cease. What happened between the appearances, and what happened after they ceased? "I am going fishing," Peter says. "We will come with you," the other disciples reply (John 21:3). Nonetheless, this life is no longer ordinary except on the surface of things. In reality it is penetrated by the other, by Christ. Christ's desire and his love had sometimes rendered his presence visible and tangible. What now explains his disappearance if not the same desire and love? The eye that has seen Christ waits for a new and definitive encounter, the Parousia. Yet, meanwhile it discovers little by little that this waiting modifies the vision it has of other people and of the things that surround it. These too are waiting but also dimly transfigured. Nothing is like it was. What will be, when the risen Lord appears again, is already penetrating and mysteriously transforming what is. The appearances of Christ prepared and began the future appearance of human beings and the world, which the Spirit is transforming into what they will be at the end.

The Supper of the Lord: The Link between Times

In his resurrection appearances Jesus let himself be seen. In this way, and together with the gift of the Spirit, he revealed the definitive reality of human beings and of all things. Then the appearances cease. The time of vision thus ends, and the time of hearing is begun. The difference between the community of the apostles and the community of those who will come after lies entirely in this fact. The *vision* of those first witnesses becomes *word* of witness, through the word received from Christ. It is by means of this word that the future disciples of Christ through the ages will encounter what the chosen witnesses saw of Christ, of human beings, and of the world. The time of Jesus Christ manifests itself as center because it is the time of appearance and of vision. The time of the Church is the time of listening, penetrated by the Spirit. Now, the identity of the same reality, in the apostolic time of vision and in the ecclesial time of hearing, is confirmed by the fact that in both of these the memory and the waiting express themselves in the same act: the celebration of the supper of the Lord. From the very beginning, the Eucharist is the place of continuity between Jesus' time and our own.

CONCLUSION

In summary, what we were able to note in general about the impact of a human death on the group of those gathered round it seems to give real substance to the way in which the writings of the New Testament present the resurrection of Jesus. It could be said that the scriptures attest to two successive appearances and disappearances of Christ. His first appearance in his condition as man is dramatically ended by his being lifted up on the cross. His appearance in his condition as the risen one is mysteriously ended by his being lifted up to the right hand of the Father. To these successive periods there correspond the figures, both identical and different, of the community of the disciples. The apostolic community is first regathered around Jesus and then, once reestablished, it becomes witness of the risen one; for its members already carry in their bodies something of the new life bestowed by the resurrection and attested to by the Spirit. These disciples had lived with Jesus, had watched the drama of his death, and had seen his glory. The witness of this community now invites others who have experienced none of this firsthand to relive on their own level these same experiences. Received in the same Spirit, this testimony provokes others to inscribe themselves, through faith, in the gesture of offering and transfiguration made by Jesus, where he drew along with him in both suffering and glory those who had followed him. The memory of these two appearances and disappearances thus remains alive, and it continually gives life to those who submit to it and proclaim it. The Eucharist is precisely this living memory.

"Dying for Others"

PHENOMENOLOGY OF A LIFE GIVEN

Death for Others and Its Celebration

Among the deaths that we do not forget and that, on the contrary, we make every effort to remember collectively, there are the deaths we describe as death for others: death for one's country, death while caring for others during an epidemic, death in the line of duty. All of these are deaths in which the life of others was more precious to those who died than their own lives. Whether one believes in God or not, these are events from which we cannot and do not want to detach ourselves. Such deaths are kept present to the memory by a symbolic monument in the village square or on the walls of the hospital. Ceremonies take place more or less regularly to celebrate the memorial: special music, the tolling of bells, speeches, and finally, among the survivors, the symbolic sharing of food. We cannot forget these deaths, because they have been the gift of life. The fact that others have given up their lives in war or in some other context means that the life we lead is a perpetual gift from those who died. They preferred our life to their own. They ran the risk of breaking themselves off from the cycle of relations with other human beings and other things so that others could continue in this cycle. By their deaths we live. How could we forget this? Moreover, how could we live in mediocrity if our life is the fruit of their deaths?[4] This is why every speech made at the monuments of the dead involves the renewal of an engagement: if we continue to live, we must do so within perspectives that the dead could agree with, indeed, perhaps along the very lines that they themselves have traced. We can only live in this good mutual agreement because our life, the life of each one of us, is the fruit of a death for all.

The Limits of Our Rituals

Unfortunately, sometimes the celebrations of the memory of our dead have about them a squalid and hypocritical aspect. This derives from the fact that in reality we do not live in the climate of generosity and unity that our speeches evoke. We come out of habit or curiosity or as a command appearance. We are bored as we listen to a speech without energy or any concrete import. We drink a toast and then return to the mediocrity of our everyday existence, to its rivalries, its enmities, its quest for profit. Even so, the deaths remembered were really deaths, and they were "deaths for others."

Yet there is a limit even greater than this. Even when our celebrations have been beautiful in their ceremonies and meaningful for the community, they do not bring back to life those who have died. This all too evident fact has something tragic, even unbearable about it. It stands there like the defeat of life in the very place where life showed itself at its highest pitch. Never do human beings show themselves more alive than when they sacrifice their own energies so that others, many others, may live and live even better lives. Like beautiful fireworks, life is extinguished and disappears in the moment when it shows itself most glorious. It is as if it cannot attain a certain degree of intensity without being destroyed. So, the "death for others," the sacrifice of self—is it the more fleeting the more rich it is with life?

As for us, the living, who live from out of the death of others or at least because of it, how can we resolve the problem of never being able to return what once was given to us? The gift of life in the "death for others" seems to be beyond the limits of the law of exchange and the reciprocity of a covenant. Without doubt, the generosity that one day permitted us to continue to live will incite us at best to give our lives for others, albeit in lesser though still real circumstances. The memory of the death of another can thus lead to the intensification of habits of exchange between people, even to the point where perhaps one day it will be granted to someone else likewise to "die for others." Perhaps in every generation human life is the fruit of that highest pitch of life and death that only some in that generation know how to attain. Nevertheless, the scandal remains: to the dead themselves, nothing more is given. Ecclesiastes would say, "This is a great vanity and a chase after the wind."

But would the dead, for their part, want back the life we would give them if we could? What return to life could have the value and the relish of the death for others in that moment when it was fully seen and lived? When others have given away their lives to the point of dying, would they want to live again? Would they want to be reinstated into a level of exchange and alliance that would necessarily be less full, less total? Those who have given up their lives and tasted that real life is to lose oneself—how would they ever be able to take up everyday life again? In the 1930s French novelist Roger Vercel, in his novel *Captain Conan,* created a hero of the Great War who, returning from among the heroes of the first air battles, found himself after the peace regularly frequenting the Café du Commerce, all blotchy and obese. More than any demonstration, this image suggests that the one who has "died for others" would not want to come back even if he could...unless—and this is the meaning of the "spiritual sacrifice" of Christians rooted in the Eucharist—daily life could attain, moment by moment, the full quality of a total gift of life.

The Ultimate Paradox

We have arrived here at the edge of the absurd: no one has ever lived more than in that moment of "dying for others," so much so that the return to normal life, were it possible, would be ridiculous. But in that case, isn't the life procured for us by that death also ridiculous? And if the dead would want no more from life, what do we want from it as we strive to attain what is best within us?

DYING AND INVOKING

Taken by itself, the theme of "death for others" risks leading us into a solitary, stoic region. Someone has decided to die because it was necessary so that others could live. But that decision leaves unresolved the paradox—and the one who died knew this perhaps—of a life that seems to have to destroy itself in order to arrive at the highest pitch of gift. Meanwhile this gift seems to have no other result than procuring a delay for the survivors, during which they will only continue an ordinary life before dying themselves. Nonetheless, the light and the peace that surround certain deaths suggest to us that a "death for others" can achieve its full meaning if it is inserted into another dimension of death. What other dimension?

From Death to Birth

To understand this we need to see how the mystery of death as an "end" arrives at the mystery of birth, an "origin." In speaking of the nature of story I tried to show that the time of origins is somehow an absolute, something that is impossible, in the last analysis, to express in language. It is that moment in which a person really comes to be, where she is placed in an immediate relation with her father, who gives her a name, and with her mother, who gives her her first food. In order to truly come to be and to begin to use her power to act in freedom, she must learn to say "father." This amounts to accepting the fact that she receives from another, not from herself, the name by which she calls herself, which distinguishes her and locates her in relation to others. To say "mother" is to accept that never has she been fed except through the care of a woman who responded to her explicit or silent request. Whoever cannot or will not say these two words will never be able to give to others their name or to provide them with food. In short, every authentic life presupposes a renunciation of total independence. It is a "submission" in which the apparent curtailing of freedom is in fact vital energy.

From the Invocation of God to the Acceptance of Death

Consenting to the dependence and interdependence signified in the names "father" and "mother" is necessary to free us for life and to allow encounters with others. But however necessary it may be, it is not the deepest consent that will be demanded of us. It is also necessary to learn how to say "Father" to the one from whom all fatherhood in heaven and on earth receives its name (Eph 3:15), to the one who gives us our being and our name, "human being." Now, this invocation of God as "Father" in thanksgiving and in acknowledgment of who God is in truth, implies paradoxically a consenting to death or—what amounts to the same thing—a giving back of our life to the one who gave it to us. This being and this name "human being" are in fact a being and a name placed in the flesh: the human being is inserted into a material world and the world of nature. Such a world is a rhythm not only of life but also of death. To be a human, therefore, it is necessary to consent to death. Neither the father who gave us our name, nor the mother who gave us to eat, nor anyone else who might appear on the scene, can grant us the power to escape from death. Thus, we cannot call God "Father" without at the same time consenting to our death, for this death derives from the creation whose origin is God.[5]

Yet perhaps this naming by God and our consenting to all that it implies are in fact a way to life. If so, its two founding times would be the following: (1) accepting our radical origin in God and (2) relying on God for the ultimate outcome of our life, which in fact is not in our power, given that we are part of the natural rhythms of life and death. Such consent would perhaps be the greatest use of human freedom, and it would undergird all other uses of free will. We have no solution to the problem of death; it stands as an obstacle to our thirst for life. Yet since this thirst does not come from ourselves alone but from the life that never ceases to spring up from inner depths of which we are not the master, then we can rely in our death on the same one from whom we receive our life. To hand over one's death as well as one's life—this is saying "my Father" to God. It is recognizing that I am the fruit of God's most intimate desire, and I trust in that desire. Thus, when a life has been lived within this consent, at the moment of death when the weakened body scarcely is able any longer to relate to others, this person finds himself once again in the place of origins, but now with his whole life story behind him and his free will still in his hands. The life that he has received so mysteriously— today he can give it back in a free gesture of his will. Consenting to death, accepting the essential name and the invocation of the name "Father," is to wait for a new name and a new body, unknown as yet, but hoped for. This final invocation is the ultimate dimension of death, and it spreads a luminous peace over the one who is leaving us.

Dying "For" Others and Giving One's Life Back "To" God

The transfiguration of death thus derives from its immediate contact with the absolute from whom its origin derived. The one dying gives her life back "to" God, and all those "for whom" she dies are given back with her. Would a "dying for" be possible without there being, at least implicitly, a "giving back to" the one who can render this sacrifice effective of some new life? In any case, we believe that the Father—having given at the beginning the name and the being that are expressed in the name received from the parents—will give a new name to the one who gives her life back to him. This new name was from the beginning the whole reason for her birth. And so, the death "for others" loses some of its paradox when it is referred to this Father "to whom" it has been given over. It would lose its paradox altogether if there were in the world a life whose death had been total transfiguration at the heart of destruction, a death not only whose sacrifice gave to the living the possibility of continuing for a little while an ordinary existence, but which raised them beyond themselves even in their everyday rhythms. But is this not exactly what the death of Jesus Christ was?

"We Proclaim Your Death, Lord Jesus"

In the liturgy we proclaim the death of Christ because it was "a death for" us: "This is my body, *which will be given up for you....*This is my blood...*It will be shed for you and for all."* But our acclamation goes beyond a joyous celebration that recognizes with thanksgiving this "for us." The Creed says that Jesus gave his life "for our salvation." But he gave it "*to* his Father." We must also reflect on this.

THE DEATH OF JESUS AND THE INVOCATION OF GOD

Jesus did not die on a glorious field of battle or in a sickbed. His cross had nothing spectacular about it. He was a prophet put to death for religious subversion that had dangerous political consequences. No one truly knew that he "died for others."[6] His own followers hardly seem to have considered his death that of a hero whose memory would hold them together for the continuation of his perilous work. Some among them, perhaps even all of them, experienced the aftertaste of a tragedy in which they knew themselves to be silent accomplices. Nonetheless, on his cross, isolated from all others and apparently having no common future with them, Jesus kept on his lips the invocation of God: "Father, into your hands I commend my spirit." It is precisely here, I think, that the meaning of Jesus' death is revealed to us. It seems to have been the place of the absolute invocation of God. He said "Father" not only with his lips and his heart but with his whole body, and he said it at that moment when to continue to live would have meant betrayal of God, the interruption of invocation, and the intentional forgetting of the name Father. Jesus did not die all at once; his death was long and drawn out. This was to give us time to understand. Jesus' death cannot be defined at the most basic level as the "violent separation of the soul from the body." Rather, it is the moment where the body, even more than the voice, accomplishes the act of invocation, thrust toward God in its own "consummation."

In speaking of the meal and especially of the invitation to the meal, I attempted to show that these were a symbol in which we spontaneously discover that the life of others is part of our own lives. We give from our own provisions so that others may live, and we prefer to receive life from others rather than from ourselves. This covenant process calls for its highest pitch: that all our being—body, soul, and spirit—be life for others and, reciprocally, that in all our being we receive life from others. Next, in speaking of language, I attempted to show the primacy of invocation, which is at one and the same time recognition and creation of the other. For this reason we all have the desire to be named personally, for without this we could not live. And so we begin to dream of an invocation so complete that it could epitomize in one single name everything that human beings could recount, invent, and construct with their language. Precisely here the death of Jesus is revealed to us as a total act in which voice and body are one in the invocation, not of another human being, but of God.

THE MEANING OF THE RESURRECTION

We can thus begin to perceive what the resurrection might mean. It obviously cannot be a restoration to life as it was lived before death. We have seen that this would not even make sense on the level of a human death "for others." By his death Jesus arrived at the plenitude of pure invocation in which he thrust his whole being toward God. Would he be able to come back to less? Nor could resurrection mean simply the memory of a moving and efficacious "death for others" that enabled us to continue our ephemeral lives. It is not the gathering of the disciples of Jesus around a monument that attests to his death and defines for us a way of living until the time comes when we too have to die. So what is it, and wherein lies its mystery?

Resurrection: Another Name for the "Death for Others"

The resurrection can be seen first of all as a consecration or a stabilization of that perfect moment of life that Jesus' death was. Death cannot really be dying when we see it for what it essentially is; namely, the ultimate gift of life in a perfect invocation. How could this free and full thrust out of oneself for the sake of others ever cease to be? Is it possible that mere appearances tell all and that this perfect movement vanishes in the same instant it is accomplished? In a first time, certainly, a rupture was necessary, and the fullness of love could only be expressed by the sacrifice.[7] But the resurrection signifies that there is a second and definitive time to this self-emptying: the transfigured being expresses in a permanent way, beyond destruction, the perfect invocation. Jesus has become invocation. The condition of the risen one is a condition in which all the powers of being are now reconciled and united in a never-ending participation in the covenant with God. So, it is not possible to imagine the risen one in a static condition, finally come to quiet and rest after that explosion of effort that lasted until the death itself. If the risen one is established anywhere at all, it is within that imperishable dynamic of his invocation of the Father into which he entered entirely and forever.

Resurrection: Invocation of the Son by the Father

Yet no one, including Christ, can establish this dynamic by himself. The man who has "died for others" has really given up his life to the point of the radical dissolution of his being. It does not pertain to him to renew the bonds that he has broken. But it is exactly this totality of the gift that calls for a response. If the invocation has been perfect, how could it not then be heard? If the invocation was a gift of life to the point of complete emptying, would not the response be life in return to the point of its complete transfiguration? The covenant is not a motionless structure. It lives from God, Creator of the world and Father of Jesus Christ; and it is from God that it becomes the law of all reality, cosmic and human, by means of the exchanges that it establishes. The resurrection is the response of God to the invocation by Christ, and it definitively establishes in him the infinite and unending exchange between God and humankind. "I have said, 'You are my Son; today I have begotten you.'" The resurrection is the definitive transfiguration of the human being—spirit, soul, and body—at the heart of that living reality that the scriptures (using primordial images) call air, fire, water: the Holy Spirit.

In this way the resurrection resolves the paradoxes that we discovered in speaking about "death for others." We have seen that those who have "died for others"—thereby bringing their lives to the highest possible human and spiritual pitch—would not want to come back to a lesser life. But if the resurrection establishes Jesus permanently within the dynamic of his final act—his offering of himself to God for all his brothers and sisters in the human race—then it is not a lesser life. It is, rather, the fulfillment of the life that was rendered perfect by its death. And if his was "a death for us," then the life that is transmitted to us through his resurrection is not merely a continuation of our ephemeral life—though it is also that—but it is already transfiguration of this life. And life's least little moments can from this point forward participate in the fullness of the resurrection. That is, what we do in this life can also signify, also realize the pure offering of the people of God for all human beings. Therefore the thanksgiving offered to the one who died for us and to the one who gave us this savior is possible on the same level as the fullness of life established by the resurrection. The cycle of exchange can be enclosed within a never-ending dynamic. The living memory of the one who died for us is the sacrificial space that opens ever anew in every generation. And so we see how the Eucharist, story and meal, can become the place where in Christ new life is ceaselessly exchanged between God and human beings, between one human being and another.

Notes

1. We could offer two comments here. On the one hand, Luke probably composed this story to throw into relief the meaning of the eucharistic celebration of the community to whom he was

addressing his gospel. On the other hand, the gospel accounts themselves of the death and resurrection could have had a liturgical *Sitz im Leben.*

2. See St. Augustine: "The glory of Christians is not their believing in Christ dead but in Christ risen." Cited, with other texts of Augustine by B. Studer, *Gratia Dei—Gratia Christi bei Augustinus von Hippo* (Rome, 1993), 89 n. 79.

3. For my part, I believe that the appearances of Jesus actually took place. This corresponds to the religious mentality of the world in which his disciples lived, who had not been introduced to modern criticism. Was not this education by appearance/disappearance the best means Christ had of awakening faith in his resurrection? I shall try to analyze its significance here.

4. At the end of Steven Spielberg's film *Saving Private Ryan,* Ryan comes as an old man on pilgrimage to the cemetery where the men whose deaths saved his life were buried. With emotion and anxiety he turns toward his wife and says, "Tell me that I lived well." How could he have lived poorly when others, young like him, had died so that he could live? How could we live poorly if Christ died for us? And yet...

5. I do not consider here for the moment the question of the relation between sin and death, but only the fact that death is in itself a natural condition and as such an element of creation. All the things God has done to let human beings escape from death, either before or after sin, do not eliminate this essential relationship between life and death for the beings on this earth. Whatever the concrete situation of a person may be, one must consent to this essential relation. We accept that God has made it this way and that our relation to God implies acceptance of our own death.

6. Except perhaps Caiaphas, if historical value is to be accorded to the remark recorded at John 11:50.

7. The question of sacrifice as a necessary dimension of freedom and the place where freedom goes beyond itself requires developments that I do not undertake here. It is a question that has always been at the center of my theological reflection.

CHAPTER FIVE

The Body and the Blood

Throughout this book I have highlighted the great symbols of exchange or covenant: a "death for others," conjugal union, and an invitation to a meal. Though human beings are full of the desire to be, they are nonetheless, despite appearances, not moved by the desire to be alone. Rather, they long for their entire being to become a giving of life to others. They long to possess nothing except what they have received from others. This intention to give and receive life finalizes human existence from within, and it drives, unconsciously perhaps, the whole history of humanity. Death, sex, and food are the great symbols of this desire. They express it, and in part they realize it. Yet it does not belong to their symbolic constitution to realize it fully.

Within and Beyond Symbols

We spoke above about the limit of the symbol of "dying for others." Those who give their lives for others attain the totality of gift and, consequently, something of the infinite. Yet to the extent that we cannot give back to them what has been given to us, the symbol has a unilateral dimension about it. Even if it remains something hoped for, covenant is not achieved in its totality. In contrast to "death for others," the symbol of invitation to the meal does effectively realize the reciprocity essential to exchange. Each person at a meal and all of them together give to one another. Here the limit lies in what is exchanged. Food bespeaks the total gift of life, but it does so in an ephemeral way.

The death and resurrection of Christ are not trapped within this limitation of the "death for others," however. We saw in the preceding chapters that they establish the situation of total exchange that is the object of human desire. If, then, they qualify the meal that remembers them, would they not also empower it somehow to go beyond its own limitations? This is precisely the faith of the church. We believe that the eucharistic meal has the same structure of reciprocity as the paschal mystery of Jesus and that it is the place where this mystery is manifested and communicated. This happens in such a way that we too can realize in its celebration all that is implied by our body and by our name: that we must give away our life to receive it back transfigured.

Transignification and Transfinalization

It is first of all by means of the word—specifically, that of the eucharistic prayer—that our sharing of bread and wine is "invested" with the mystery of Christ and attains the signification of absolute exchange. Recent theological research has rightly tended to speak here of a "transignification of the meal": the signification of covenant inscribed in every exchange of food is here totally *de-sign-ated*.[1] The invocation of God, the evocation of the mystery of Christ, the plea for the Holy Spirit—all these *de-sign-ate* the meaning of the exchange of foods and thus bring them to signify the new and eternal covenant, established by means of the body and blood of Christ, by means of the gift of the Holy Spirit to the community.

Among all the stories that human beings tell, we drew attention to the special importance of those that recall and want to render present the founding events of origins and the end. We spoke of the absolute originality of their language. It reaches back to a past that can hardly be put into words; it anticipates a future whose shape no one knows. These events belong to all human beings; and if they share the story of these in their feasts, it is nonetheless before God that the story is recited. Here, at the level of origins and the end, the temporal projects of human beings are only at their very first budding forth or in the last moments of their final fulfillment. The exchange here is not among human beings in the interplay that forges their diversity into the composition of a particular history. No, here the exchange is with God, creator and savior. It is the founding exchange that here and now lets a human history unfold that will be the history of God with human beings. During this history we still await that lasting city whose very life will be comprised of the invocation of the name of God by the evocation of the Lamb who was slain. The only real "Feast for Humanity" can be the exchange with God. What it celebrates and actualizes is the first coming to be of human beings and their final consummation. It takes us back to our own roots and orients us toward our fulfillment. Within these poles our present life springs up filled with its truth and meaning.

The Christian Eucharist includes in its joyful invocation of God a recounting of the death and resurrection of Jesus, celebrated as the true founding event of humanity. I have tried to describe the absolute meaning of this story, a meaning bound to the paschal experience of the resurrection and to a meditation on its significance. Its significance concerns the person of Jesus, who represents us; it concerns us who enter into the "admirable exchange" consummated in him and forever alive in him. The eucharistic story addressed to God celebrates the plenitude of his gift to us and of our giving it back in Jesus Christ. It says that in Jesus all this "substance" of the world and of human beings is really taken up into the absolute dynamic of exchange between God's generosity and the pure offering made in response. It "de-signates" the place of this exchange: the body handed over and the blood poured out. Truly, then, it expands to infinite proportions the significance of the exchange inherent in every meal. In this sense it "transignifies"—and we could also say it "transfinalizes"—that is, the finality of covenant only aimed at in the exchange of every meal is *accomplished* here and now in the very moment when this meal is celebrated.

TOWARD TRANSUBSTANTIATION

Let us push these reflections further. The joyful memory of our salvation in Jesus Christ is celebrated in the interplay of words and the exchange of food. If the eucharistic story is altogether unique among all the stories that can be told, what should we say then of its food? If the *story* of a past event accomplished in Jesus Christ is told in a jubilant *present* tense, can we not say that the *meal* renders *present* the flesh and blood of the humanity of Christ that once suffered? We have seen that this suffering humanity is unique in all the world, for in it those who speak and those who eat can themselves become pure offering.

Put differently: on the level of language and of story, the eucharistic figure is unique. This absolute event cannot be celebrated in an everyday language. All the registers of the word are in fact present in the celebration. They are coordinated with one another and forge a religious poem without equal. The word uttered in time arrives, as closely as possible, at the purity and total richness of *the* Word. Will this uniqueness, achieved on the level of language, not also be found on the level of the food? In the *language,* the words, the accents, the phrases all arrive at the plenitude of Christ.

In the *food,* will not the elements be transfigured into the body handed over and the blood poured out, as the place of gift and of the resurrection? In some sense we could say that *every word* has been created so that one day a pure word of offering might be uttered and recapitulate in itself all that human beings would ever say. In the same way, have not *all foods* been created so that one day they might be taken up into a meal where the "totality"—that is, the body and blood of Christ—might be offered and exchanged between God and human beings? All the substance of the world should be able to pass into festal *meal* tuned to the *story* of the founding event: to the genesis of a new world founded in the risen Christ and coming from the hand of God there should correspond the offering of this new world coming from the hands of human beings. The sacred foods will be the mysterious place of this all-embracing exchange between God and human beings.

"Transubstantiation"

The word *transubstantiation* is meant to describe this exchange, but in fact it seems to scare us off. It is complicated and consequently not especially accessible to the average person. Above all, it evokes a metaphysics of substance and accident whose relevance is not evident to all today. It is culturally outdated if not definitively surpassed, and the highly abstract speculation that it evokes has ceased to touch our imagination. It would seem that a substitute should be found.

A Symbolic Word

Nonetheless, I would like to preserve this word, and I shall try to make clear why and to what extent. But I would like to do so by trying, first of all, to recover its emotional value and its symbolic roots. Theological words have a fairly precise meaning when we situate them within the logical systems of which they form a part, but their richness is born from an enthusiasm for the faith and from a profound sense of human beings and their symbols. The Ephesians of the fifth century shouted the strange word *Theotokos* in the streets of their city because they had invested the essence of their faith in Christ in this technically precise theological term. They did this in both a dynamic and polemical way: the Virgin Mary was proclaimed "Mother of God" against all who held that the son of Mary was a simple human being. Theologians were later able to analyze the concept of "divine maternity" by means of a very subtle understanding of the relation between Mary and her son. But the word *Theotokos* is and remains an impassioned affirmation of faith. It is undoubtedly necessary to recover the comparable climate surrounding the word *transubstantiation*.

The Middle Ages

Raymond Oursel has called *transubstantiation* the motto not of scholasticism but of the spirituality and mysticism that inspired Romanesque art. This spirituality was characterized by a very lively sense of the "marvelous exchange" between God and human beings that spread a transfiguring light over all things. The passage from human bread to the body of Christ, from wine to his blood, is its symbol, its fulfillment, the keystone of its vault.[2] Far from being a dry and narrow word, *transubstantiation* expresses the ultimate meaning of the dynamic of this whole world.

Later, the Dominican theologian and poet Thomas Aquinas composed a hymn in honor of the Blessed Sacrament called *Lauda Sion Salvatorem*. In Latin verse this hymn expresses the scholastic speculation on the "real presence" and the beautiful metaphysics it presupposes. When we read this text today, we are surprised by the dry character of this liturgical composition. But it is probably we who fail to perceive just how much the enthusiasm of the faith of our ancestors was born out of their investigation of the transformation of human elements into the body and blood of Christ. For them the love of God for humanity was manifested precisely here in this downpour of "metaphysical miracles" whose only scope was to allow human beings to participate in the mystery of Christ. What being and nature could not realize, God did. *Lauda Sion* is a hymn to the tenderness of the Almighty at pains to establish communion with his children. If we strip it of its affective intensity, it appears as nothing other than a grim treatise in uninspired verse. But it is perhaps we who have become blind to its significance.

Imagination Concerning Food

Gilbert Durand reminds us of the human roots of this emotional perception of transubstantiation. "All food is transubstantiation," he wrote *(The Anthropological Structures of the Imaginary)*. It all aims at that. This means that the imagination concerning food always tends to go beyond the aspect of its destruction, wanting to diminish this negative dimension and keep it to a minimum, in this way underscoring the passage from substance to substance. "Substance" is seen here as the heart of the food, that by which it gives life, what is transformed in some sense into the heart of the one nourished by it. From here the passage to the imagination of a primordial food is easy: a sacred drink or the fruit of paradise, a "supersubstantial" element that would give immortal life, an imperishable substance that not only (and not even principally) would be transformed into

the one who eats it, but rather would transform the one eating into itself, and so snatch him from his mortality.

Levinas

Perhaps more than anyone else today, it is Levinas who
helps us to rediscover these human roots of transubstantiation. In several pages at the end of *Totality and Infinity* he
speaks of this when, in order to move "beyond the countenance," he evokes with modesty and with force the sexual
encounter. The countenance is a place of significance; it is
gift and search for meaning. It manifests itself or is sought in
the light. In its own way it is a clear word. But beyond faces
there are bodies in their erotic nudity. Love includes and also
exchanges obscure and indispensable regions of our being.
Its gesture is not the glance but the caress. Its desire not only
aims at recognition by the other but seeks some sort of identification with the other, through feeling and pleasure that go
beyond or—what amounts to the same thing—fall short of
all significance and intelligence. Here in some sense we are
even beyond the persons themselves or any designation they
could give to themselves. Here they touch one another in an
implicit recognition, they join themselves to each other in the
bright darkness of intimacy, in a solitude involving two that
does not open itself publicly to any society. Could we say
that they attain a passage "from substance to substance"? At
this point, however, their intimacy transcends even itself; for
the loving identification produces an other: an infant conceived. Now it is precisely at this point, in speaking of fecundity, that Levinas invokes the word *transubstantiation* three
times in these pages. It is unquestionably suited to the situation. It designates, first, this passage beyond one's own substance in order to be identified with the substance of the
beloved even in the other's feelings and pleasure. It likewise

designates the generation of a child, which exceeds all planned projects and all powers under their control, and which is the passage of the substance of the lovers into the substance of another person coming forth from them. In its reality and fecundity love surpasses the domain of the intelligence, of the senses, of clear-eyed freedom, of self-mastery. It likewise surpasses the domain of the body in so far as this is only material and neediness. But if it surpasses all these, it likewise envelopes them all in a movement forward that is both consented to and blind: the lover does not find himself except in transubstantiating himself in some way in the beloved and in the fruit of their love. A dynamic gesture, this! It never finishes but is always open to a future. We could almost say that on the level of love, being is not substance except by continually transubstantiating itself.

In this way, can't the word *transubstantiation* become a little more familiar to us and a little less formidable? For it manages to express, or at least to suggest with intensity, the dynamic of conjugal desire as a need for absolute communication that is latent in the imagination concerning food and the alchemist's utopia. The word's origin is definitely theological and eucharistic. The fact that philosophers have recourse to it should accredit it anew in our eyes. It is certainly one of those overcharged locutions that we employ when we attempt to express the intimate infinity of our desire. Furthermore, it is striking that it is used both in the context of total love between woman and man and in the context of the transmutation of food and the elements. It is as if this need for union were at play not only in the context of interpersonal exchange but also in the relationship of human beings with the elements. It is as if, in the end, it were necessary to involve these two dimensions of what is human (human beings—earth and human being—human being) in order to embrace the final aim of the total human desire. It is a being with one another while also being with the earth and reciprocally being with the earth while being with others. Then this reciprocity and multiple transmutation mysteriously give way to an immortality that also involves an exchange with the world of God.

Transubstantiation thus appears as a metaphor for desire. It is a way of expressing it and in so doing of giving it a concrete context. Yet when it is used in the context of Christian Eucharist, it goes even further and surpasses that limit which is everywhere else impassible: the limit between human desire, the metaphors that give it body and sense, and the reality aimed at by the metaphors; namely, the dynamic unity of earth, human beings and God. To understand this, or at least to gain some feel for it, we must renounce considering transubstantiation only as some sort of change or even as a precise change. First we must reflect again on what it points to: the body and blood of Jesus Christ.

The Body, The Blood, and The Name

Throughout our discussion we have encountered again and again the human body and its paradox. It is truly flesh, but flesh animated by needs, crosscut with desire, formed by language as much as by material, called by a proper name that makes it a human body. It is at one and the same time "substance" and "symbol." Perhaps this condition seems paradoxical to us because we are so deeply imbued with a basic Cartesian view that makes of "body" and "soul" two incompatible "things." But the greater reason for the paradox is that our human destiny lies in the future. Our journey must still pass through death, and we do not yet know that new name that will let us at last fully become living bodies. And the story does not end before all human beings have at last totally become living bodies. We await the resurrection of the dead.

BODY AND BLOOD FULFILLED

There is one body, however, which has already reached its fulfillment, such that it is *the* body. It has not ceased to be flesh. On the contrary, it has revealed the flesh in its finally acquired truth, that of a transfiguration inscribed in the body by absolute love. If all that we have seen in the preceding chapters is true, then the human body is not truly body until it has been totally handed over and lives its standing beyond itself in the permanence of resurrection. We could also say that it becomes truly body when it is marked by the sign of blood poured out. Living persons do not see their own blood. The body protects it within as a precious tissue that accumulates and circulates life. Blood brutally poured out and thus visible is consequently a sign of death. But as life "given to" and "offered for" it is also a sign of the body "such as it will be" when love transfigures it. Blood poured out shows us that it is essential to the body that it be handed over. Only the body handed over and the blood poured out can rise again; and if after that they die no more, they still do not cease being handed over and poured out, because it is in this way that they are truly and forever the body and blood of a human being. It is thus that the full reality of the body of Jesus was revealed to us when his blood was poured out, when his side was opened. He is the Lamb who has been slain. He has become *symbol* without ceasing to be *substance* and is henceforth the master of appearing as he wishes and of drawing his disciples toward the same offering and the same resurrection.

THE BODY FINALLY NAMED

The body and blood of Jesus are thus simply *the* body and *the* blood because they alone have become what body and blood are destined to be. But they have become such because in them Christ was somehow equal to the name he bore. From the beginning he was named "Jesus," not by the wish of his parents but, through an inspired message, by God his Father. He was thus charged in his body not with the responsibility and the service attached to all names. (Recall that we are given names so that we can be invoked and called.) His was the responsibility and service attached to being the divine Son named by his divine Father. He responded in his body and in his blood and so has received "the name which is above every other name" (Phil 2:9). Jesus was not merely a human being like all others, but one who was destined to give more than all others and so destined to merit resurrection by anticipation. He is certainly a human being like all others, but much more, because his flesh, crosscut by his condition as divine Son and invested with his role as messiah, is destined to establish the kingdom of God, which is totally contained in the name by which both God and human beings invoke him and call him.

I am simply repeating here what I have tried to suggest everywhere in these pages. I have been repeatedly speaking about food and language. We have seen it at every turn: body and name go together. Now, if the name is such that it could respond at any time either to a call from the Almighty God or from the least among human beings, then the body that carries that name can also respond for all bodies and the blood respond for all blood. Conversely, if in his body and in his name Christ responds for us, then our body and our name can be marked by a reference to Christ through which they attain to their true dimensions, that of covenant with

God. As I said above, the risen Christ does not reestablish his community on old, preparatory, and provisional foundations. He establishes it by offering participation in a new and definitive life, that of his self-emptying in death and the new fullness of resurrection. Our bodies, our blood, our names are not simply counted alongside the body, the blood, and the name of Jesus. Rather, ours are referred to his, as parts to the whole, as members to the body, as sons and daughters in the Son. The mystery of the Church as the body of Christ is included *within* the mystery of Christ risen in his body. It is the same reality seen from different points of view.

THIS BREAD AND THIS WINE...

In celebrating the Eucharist, we want to give thanks in faith and in the Holy Spirit for this mystery of the body and blood of Christ, for we are deeply implicated in it. By committing ourselves to this mystery, we want also to ratify in some way our being implicated in it. This is why *we* bring to the Eucharist bread and wine, "fruit of the earth and work of human hands." They are symbols of humanity, not only in its static materiality, but in the dynamism of its work. They are symbols also of the necessary communication among human beings so that this work can be accomplished and its fruits shared. Finally, they are symbols of the constant sacrifice in which all human beings must continually invite their neighbors to take what is theirs for living and to give to others what they have. All these dimensions included in the total symbolism of the meal are present already in the bringing of bread and wine. We cannot come before God empty-handed, for we were created in order to give all to the point of death and resurrection. We cannot come before him without all our brothers and sisters, by whom we are bodies and who are bodies through us. Above all, we cannot come before God without Christ. This is why in the eucharistic offering, when we hand over our bodies to God in the invocation of his name, we include all human beings, and above all we do it in the name of Jesus or—*what amounts to the same thing!*—in his body and blood, which are *the* body and *the* blood. This is also why an insistent intercession begs that these offerings "become" the body and blood of Jesus Christ—not as some inert piece of matter but as the living substances of the gift of life in the paschal mystery.

...SO THAT THEY MAY BECOME THE BODY AND BLOOD OF OUR LORD JESUS CHRIST

Understood in this perspective, the idea of our bread and wine "becoming" something else during the eucharistic meal really should not surprise or disturb us. The memorial of the death and resurrection of Jesus is prayed and celebrated on the level of the primordial events of origins and end. The words achieve the transignification of the meal. But this could not happen without the transubstantiation of the food, so that between God and us (on the level of things and of saying, on the level of doing and of speaking) there should be nothing but the body and blood of Christ. How could there be anything else? How—between God and us—could there be anything other than this body and this blood?

I wish to insist: we cannot isolate transubstantiation from the human desire that speaks this word or from the precise objects in reference to which it is said. The word *transubstantiation* is not one of those generic words that can be applied to multiple situations as the case may be. Rather, on the level of the dynamic relationship of human beings to the things of this world, it indicates the desire for the absolute transmutation that guarantees access to the definitive. The word cannot be thrown around as if it were applicable to any kind of "substance." Even if it is used metaphorically, as we saw above in the discussion of Levinas' use of the term, in the strict sense it only applies to the mysterious change of human bread into the unique body of Jesus Christ, the change of human wine into his blood, so that this body and blood might be definitively exchanged between God and human beings. The dynamic of reciprocal gift that human desire has felt from the beginning is effectively realized in the mystery of Christ commemorated here and now.

In other words, a universal transmutation is nothing but a myth, in the pejorative sense of that term. It really doesn't mean anything. But the transubstantiation of bread into the body of Christ and of wine into his blood, taken within the definitive dynamic of the death and resurrection of Jesus, does mean something. We could even say it *is all meaning*. And so, we cannot speak of transubstantiation only thinking of the "things" that are changed (e.g., a piece of bread into a bio-physical body). We have to take account of what each is. The one is the fruit of human labor and the possible place of exchange in the meal offered. The other is, by the Word of God, the whole of created reality transfigured by the resurrection and taken up into an eternal communion with God. Implicated in this marvelous and unique exchange, transubstantiation correctly says and effects an aspect of the mystery: the passage from a human reality into the divine-human reality that human beings have sought, from the beginning, to attain and that is given to them in the Eucharist so that they in turn can offer it back.

OBJECTIONS

It must be admitted, however, that in recent years in discussions concerning *real presence* and *transubstantiation*, this latter term has experienced an eclipse. In the context of ecumenical dialogue, especially with that of the Reformation, and also in light of a current disaffection with any metaphysic considered as an "ontotheology," attempts have been made, when analyzing the eucharistic mystery, to replace the category of substance with the categories of finality, sign, and symbol. In the same context of ecumenical dialogue, especially with the Orthodox, there has been an insistence on the role of the Holy Spirit rather than on the nature of the act that the Spirit accomplishes. But I wonder if some resistance to such trends should not be offered. Would it not be more useful to "distinguish in order to unite"? It seems to me it is not so much a problem with finding substitutes or replacements as a question of trying to put each element in its place within the poetic movement of the mystery of faith. From this point of view it is absolutely necessary to recognize that ecumenical discussion invites us to accord priority to the dimension of covenant. Here covenant would be considered as inscribed within the entire Christian mystery; it is transformed within this mystery because it responds to the deepest desires of human beings. In this regard *transignification, transymbolization, transfinalization* are the most relevant categories. It is also necessary to admit that the Catholic insistence on the role of the priest in the eucharistic celebration has consigned to the background the role of the Spirit through whom everything is worked. Concerning the priest, at most we could say that his role is instrumental, that is, dependent and derived. It is for this reason that I insisted on the language of intercession and the role of the epiclesis in the eucharistic liturgy. This is in line with recent liturgical studies. Nothing happens in the liturgy apart from the power of God. Once all this is granted, however, is it still not also necessary to speak of the action itself in all its aspects and in particular in that aspect that concerns bread and wine becoming Christ's body and blood? After all, all the ancient traditions of the Church concerned themselves with this. At this precise point the language of "transubstantiation" is legitimate. In effect it qualifies the "becoming" that happens in the Eucharist. It indicates what true "becoming" is—different from all other forms of becoming and transformation that we might be able to imagine.

Certainly, doubts could be raised concerning the validity of one or another understanding of the concept of "substance." Yet this "substantive" (to call it by its grammatical name) exists and it is widely employed in current language. So surely it says something. Besides, it would be flippant to maintain that the intense philosophical reflection around this term from Plato to our own day no longer has anything to say to us.

Indeed, it designates that which is the *invariable* in reality. The problem of the invariable and all variables is inescapable in any epoch. The Nobel Prize-winning biochemist Jacques Monod faced this problem head on in the context of modern science: "There is and there will remain in science a Platonic element that could not be eliminated without destroying it. In the infinite diversity of individual phenomena, science always seeks an invariable" *(Chance and Necessity)*. I believe that this "Platonic element" remains in philosophy just as it does in science. For what concerns the Eucharist, it is on this level that the concept of transubstantiation must be located. St. Thomas Aquinas attempts to speak of such notions as real presence and transubstantiation in pages that are full of nuance, metaphysical subtlety, and intellectual modesty. We may not be inclined to put such an approach at the center of our own reflection on the Eucharist today. And yet on their own level and for approaching the meaning of faith in what concerns the precise question of what the food "becomes," his reflections are perfectly worthy of adherence.[3] It may be the case that today we do not experience as much as we used to the need to treat the problem of transubstantiation in detail. Yet it does not seem proper to discard the notion outright or to reject immoderately the way in which some of our greatest forbears posed this in such a central way for the reflection of believers.

We can conclude this chapter by saying that according to this double line of transignification and transubstantiation it is possible to gain some feeling for the way in which the mystery of the death and resurrection of Christ invades the simple meal of bread and wine that we exchange in the presence of God as we make a memorial of Christ. Unique among all exchanges and all sharing of food, the Eucharist realizes what it signifies: the complete covenant between God and human beings. In virtue of this covenant given and celebrated, the next step would be continually to reopen a history that realizes all the projects of the human being, who alone among all creatures stands upright and is active in the production of food. But such a history will move forward from the Eucharist in such a way that it always opens further to new possibilities of realizing the unique covenant. This is the true "Feast of Humanity."

Notes

1. In what follows I use different forms of these somewhat difficult and clumsy words—transignification, transfinalization, transubstantiation, signification, substance—in an attempt to see the value of the traditions and current discussions that have used them.

2. Raymond Oursel, *Floraison de la sculpture romane,* vol. 2 (Paris: Zodiaque, 1976), 233–47.

3. A distinction is necessary, however. The word *transubstantiation* itself stands in fact at the limit of possible language. It is

nearly negative theology: since it cannot be a question of a localized movement, of a qualitative movement, or of generation-corruption, then it must be a change from "substance to substance," without our being able to say much more about it. Further speculations about "the subsistence of the accidents in the quantity" can be accepted by those who have affinity for this type of metaphysical reasoning, but they are not necessary for the acceptance of transubstantiation as an adequate expression of eucharistic "becoming."

Conclusion

One basic conviction has guided this entire essay. It under-girds all its developments and was made explicit from time to time. If I were to say it with just one word, it would be *transfiguration*. Human existence presents a number of concrete faces, behaviors, and actions—"figures"—that no authentic religion can deny or even simply ignore. These are food, work, sex, suffering, and death. All the registers of the human voice and word correspond to these. These figures call to one another and respond to one another. None of them, however, is perfect; that is, none completely satisfies the personal or collective desire of human beings. Each and all point in the same direction, but none attains its goal. That is why they remain open. They summon what they signify and only partially reach it. They are summoning something or someone else that they do not know and cannot produce but that nonetheless responds better than they themselves to what they seek. They summon their own "transfiguration."

It was necessary, therefore, to consider these figures: what they are and what they do, what they say and what questions they raise. This was all the more necessary because in Christianity the response of God to the hope of these figures invites us to take up again our most familiar activities, but on a level where their definitive sense is suddenly revealed and given. The Eucharist: at one and the same time it is feast and death, word of invocation and story, life and communion!

This is why we began by looking at food as a concrete function (virtually the first concrete function), but also as an activity that reveals human beings to themselves precisely because it is the first concrete function. Food manifests to human beings their biological rootedness; and, because it furnishes them with the foundation of their language, it also manifests their symbolic capacity. The human being is inseparably substance and symbol. As the fruit of labor that produces "subsistences," food reveals to humans their technical power and simultaneously its aesthetic requirements. It displays the collective dimension of humanity, for no one makes food or works for it or consumes it alone and for oneself. A just sharing on the level both of work and of distributing its fruits appears here as the fundamental law that should regulate all human projects and their realization. However, the common experience of a gratuitous invitation to a meal manifests on this most basic level of food a profound human desire, inexplicable perhaps, but latent in our every move: the desire to give life without counting the cost and to receive it with all our defenses dropped. The law of exchange and covenant is more radical still than the law of just sharing. The overabundance of the feast is more fundamental than equal sharing. And in this way food poses the true theoretical and practical problem of human existence: how to coordinate the project of justice and the desire for covenant? Here also, then, the fundamental poverty of humanity is likewise revealed: who will give the covenant unreservedly to human beings, the covenant where everything is given and everything is received?

In its turn, the word also reveals the human being. It immediately shows the human person to be a being of communion. There are no words except words exchanged. And the word defines the symbolic field of communion: music. Each one of us is a voice for others—a song and melody.

Meanings, themes, ideas—all pass through the interpersonal poetic of human beings addressing themselves to one another. If it happens that someone speaks without addressing another, nothing really has been said. The words fall like overripe fruit that no one gathers. The opposite is also true. When there is nothing offered in a word, it is empty and insignificant. The offering of silence has more meaning than senseless chatter.

The desire for communion also manifests itself on the level of content. This is clearest in the story, that most frequent context for the use of words and the child of memory. To tell a story is to take up a past event, near or far, and render it the property of those to whom it is told. To listen to it is to make our own what we ourselves have not lived. In this way we realize a communion among our diversities so that we can live the present together and project a future. This is the framework, many times a day, in which the "history" unfolds that brings to the present of our collective consciousness all the past that has made us what we are and from which we can design what we will be. Here again a delicate reciprocity is woven between the project of present communion and the fidelity with which memory discerns and presents past events. Projects and contents condition each other.

Among all the stories that can be told, what stands out are those that treat of life given, shared, and handed back. Such stories keep coming back. We are never finished remembering life. And such stories are not neutral. They are either feast or mourning. Birth or death, marriage, an inauguration, a completion—it doesn't matter, in the end the basic story always points to the origin and to the end. These are the limit places of life. Without our evoking these, what happens in between has no meaning and cannot be directed anywhere. So, ultimately the story reaches back and touches our first naming, and it reaches forward and anticipates our death. For our birth is epitomized in the name that was given us, and our death is our last invocation and final listening for a word of response. In the same way, every particular story is inscribed within the larger framework of the primordial story that recounts the origins and anticipates the end. Now, whether particular or universal, such a story brings us to the poem. If every invocation is necessarily particular, this particularity is inserted within the duration of time; but the evocation of the origin and the end attaches a word to what founds time and what in some sense ends it. Its language is thus unique, at once human and surpassing what is human. And if this evocation is also invocation of the one to whom the story is told, as is all evocation, then to whom is the primordial story told if not to the one who first gave names to the worlds and to human beings and with whom therefore communion has become possible? God the Creator and Father! It is this that I wanted to express in saying that the founding discourse is the liturgical poem: a song addressed to God, a response to the name that God has given, a passing beyond merely human limits.

But where, concretely, can we find this language of origins implicit in every human word? Christians believe that the celebration of the Eucharist in a community of brothers and sisters is the primordial and ultimate voice. It sings an invocation of God that evokes the first and last event: the death and resurrection of Jesus of Nazareth, the Christ. Eucharist is language of origins first of all because it invokes God in a jubilant acclamation of his name: Father. It is a founding word because it evokes what God has done for human beings, his project of salvation accomplished in Jesus Christ. Because it tells a story and because it does so in memory of and at the command of the one who was dead and now lives forever, the Eucharist renders present in its thanksgiving what it evokes. The Eucharist says, here and now, that event from which all that extends in time finds its meaning and from which every history can be constructed in an intelligible way.

But the Eucharist is more than a word, even if it is a founding word. Or put more exactly: it is word in the active sense, a "performative" word, as would be said today. This is the sense of the Hebrew word *davar.* The invocation and evocation are pronounced over things and with gestures in a plea for the power of the Holy Spirit who alone is able to give body to our signs. The reality of the things in front of us gives consistency to the words that come from our lips. The dimension of presence, already marked by the here-and-now invocation of God and the here-and-now evocation of Jesus Christ, becomes incarnate in these things. The Spirit, transfiguring the things, renders present the event of salvation, the true origin and end of all history. And this is not a performance that passes before our eyes and leaves us out. It is we who do the invoking, we who tell the story, we who do again what the Lord commanded. In this way we too are included in the covenant that we celebrate in word and with food. Thus, not only are we assured of the origin and the end, but we are already taken up into them, framed by them. Without these, it is impossible for human beings to live, for they have not yet overcome the terror of what surpasses them and of what they cannot give themselves. The presence of these "ultimates"—origin and end—accompanying each moment of time and each portion of space, paradoxically allows us to live in a particular time and particular space with a constructive freedom. Freed from uncertainty and fear, we can risk the future.

The Christian cannot prove that the death and resurrection of Jesus are effectively the founding event that makes life possible. This is precisely the object of faith. This is a word *(dabar)* from God. Now, a word is listened to and obeyed. It is neither invented nor proved. It is possible, however, without putting the word in doubt, to seek to penetrate its truth. It can be "verified," not in the sense that its truth would depend on our verification, but simply because it might appear clearer to us by means of our modest attempts. Among many possible ways of verification, I have attempted to offer two here.

The first is the Church of Jesus. Its very existence verifies the resurrection. It is continually being born from a hearing of the apostolic witness. This witness is a word in which those who were dispersed by the death of Jesus explain why, contrary to all expectations, they remained together and began to speak. They did so because the one who had died let himself be seen again, without initiative on their part, without their being able to lay hands on him at will. And yet they could not doubt his identity, and the one who let himself be seen commissioned them to speak. The Church is thus entirely dependent on this manifestation of Jesus after his death (identical and different) and the mission that accompanied it. In its very being the Church likewise manifests this strange combination of a dimension full of humanity and a mystery that surpasses it and without which it would not be. The Church is the first fruits of the new creation, sent to tell other human beings who they are in truth, and the servant of transfiguration, the community of the risen one. The death and resurrection of Jesus are thus unveiled as the event by which the entire creation gradually arrives at its ultimate meaning. This is the first "verification."

The second emerges from the paradox of the "death for others." Certainly, it is true, as Aragon said in a ballad on the glory of the heroes of the Resistance, "the one who believed in God and the one who didn't believe" were both able to give their lives with equal generosity and elicit equal admiration. Yet would it really be possible to "verify" the death of these men for their brothers and sisters if there were not a Father who could receive their sacrifice and respond to it, thereby establishing the infinite circle of covenant in which death is life and life is death? The resurrection of Christ breaks through the paradox of the "death for others" because it inserts the one who gave his life and does not receive it back for himself into the impetuous dynamism of exchange between God and human beings. At this level Christ is origin and end because in him life has at last become what it was called to be. Without being closed, it is accomplished. Set forever "in orbit," it is the end. Appearing now for what it is and communicated to all who wish to receive it and be taken up into its dynamism, it is origin. No other human life has ever realized this. This is the second verification.

As I suggested, from these verifications there springs up the need to reflect on the One who is both at the origin and the end. Who is he? Here the theological question about Jesus Christ is born. And it can be infinitely developed, provided that the response in each moment of history is faithful to what gave it birth: the event of death and resurrection as the origin and end of time, of the world, of history.

If the death and resurrection of Jesus of Nazareth are truly the unique event that is the origin and end of history, it becomes easier to understand the extent to which they invade not only the discourse but the gestures and things used to commemorate them in the solemn and joyful invocation of God as Father. We have seen that in itself the festal meal is the suitable symbol of reciprocal gift, of sacrifice in its fullness, where all is given and all is received. The festal meal of the Eucharist is charged with the reality it signifies. This is not a Platonic ideal located in a world above us, nor is it a utopian event of an imagined future. It is the event of

Jesus Christ here and now recalled to memory and called into reality. I have underlined it a number of times: the meal perfectly *said* covenant, in the same way that the death and resurrection *did* the covenant and still *do* it. The combination of these in the eucharistic discourse and its food confers on the food the plenitude of what is evoked in the discourse. "Transubstantiation" is the ultimate seal of this presence, not an inert presence, a static and impotent being there, but the presence of the covenant, offered to the hand and the mouth of human beings. It is offered so that human life might be transfigured and develop within the duration of time ways of acting worthy of this condition of Son, which is for us the ultimate name of the covenant.

The covenant and the condition of being Son open the duration of time and render history possible. The covenant thwarts death by revealing its meaning. It establishes a dynamic relation with God. It stands under the banner of love as reciprocal exchange. For these reasons it can break the tendency, ever alive, to go backwards, to recoil into the past or to take off toward some world that has nothing to do with our own. Because the covenant delivers the ultimate meaning of being and of things, it provides the framework within which the unfolding of time finds its reason for being and its models. In this way covenant opens onto human projects of development, of justice, of sharing.

The expression "brothers and sisters" is that which, for good or for ill, designates a human action undertaken together or a situation of sharing. We willingly envision a "more just and fraternal" world from which all rivalries and injustice would be banished and where differences would be held in harmony. But are not brothers and sisters by definition all children of the same father? They have accepted not only being engendered by him, but also that their father has shared among them all his tenderness and goods. If the celebration of the new covenant is the confession of the name Father, this founds the family of human beings and opens onto ways of action and struggle so that this family may be effectively realized. Because the covenant makes us brothers and sisters, its celebration provokes us to work to be so more equitably. It is the point of departure for the struggle for justice.

It also gives this struggle its final sense. To share, to be equal—but why? So that everyone can have as much as everyone else, the same amount of material and cultural goods, and do with them whatever is wished? But who would maintain this state of perfect equality, supposing it could be achieved? "In the beginning was Jealousy," a myth from Gabon says. The only way to maintain a static equality would be to work hard to keep anyone from surpassing the common denominator! Hardly an engaging project! But this is not how it is meant to be. If it is important that justice grow stronger and be more widespread, the reason is to permit all to have enough so that they may give it away, spread it around, and be lavish with what they have. It would mean also in another moment a situation where they would sit down at table and receive from others, without bringing anything themselves, because they have already given all away and it is now their time to receive.

In reality the concrete life of human beings is or ought to be a mixture of sharing and exchange, of justice and covenant. Political discourses that trace an ideal of justice often surpass their own premises and suggest, without putting it into words, attitudes and practices that actually belong to covenant and to sacrifice. It would be difficult to accomplish anything without such attitudes and practices. Conversely, the word of covenant includes the "law of freedom," for it is not possible to confess God as Father without loving others as oneself. To be effective, such a love must give rise to the reflections and concrete projects needed so that every human being can take the upright stance that belongs to us all.

It is not my intention to pursue this theme at length. To conclude this book I want simply to put in relation to one another all that we have spoken about here: on the one hand, covenant, the reality of origins and of end continually present to humanity through the Eucharist (the true "Mass on the Altar of the World"), and on the other hand, sharing, the reality of development, of becoming, of time, and so of work and of politics. I do not believe that covenant can be tacked on to "the end" of sharing as an appendix that would render its approaches holy. At the same time, I do not think that covenant can close in on itself and never penetrate the concrete time of those who celebrate it, thereby also reaching those who do not celebrate it. Instead, the concrete combination of covenant and sharing at each moment of time—this is the common task of us all.

References

Derrida, Jacques. *Of Grammatology.* Baltimore: Johns Hopkins University Press, 1976.

Derrida, Jacques. *Speech and Phenomena, and Other Essays on Husserl's Theory of Signs.* Evanston, IL: Northwestern University Press, 1973.

Detienne, Marcel, and Jean-Pierre Vernant. *The Cuisine of Sacrifice among the Greeks.* Chicago: University of Chicago Press, 1998.

Durand, Gilbert. *The Anthropological Structures of the Imaginary.* Brisbane, Australia: Boombana, 1999.

Eliade, Mircea. *Myths, Dreams, and Mysteries; the Encounter between Contemporary Faiths and Archaic Realities.* New York: Harpercollins, 1961.

Lévinas, Emmanuel. *Autrement qu'être et au-delà de l'essence.* La Haye, 1974.

Lévinas, Emmanuel. *Totality and Infinity: An Essay on Exteriority.* Pittsburgh: Duquesne University Press, 1969.

Lévi-Strauss, Claude. *The Elementary Structures of Kinship.* Boston: Beacon Press, 1971.

Monod, Jacques. *Chance and Necessity.* New York: Knopf, 1971.

Ricoeur, Paul. *Fallible Man: Philosophy of the Will.* Chicago: Regnery, 1965.